ONE BLOODY ROAD

THE GLORIOUS WAY OF DISCIPLESHIP

J.G. GARRETT

Copyright © 2016 by J.G. Garrett
Burning Ones

One Bloody Road
by John Garrett

Printed in the United States of America

ISBN: 978-0-9976345-0-1

All rights reserved. No part of this document may be reproduced or transmitted in any form, by any means (electronic, photocopying, recording, or otherwise) without the written permission of the author.

Unless otherwise indicated, Bible quotations are taken from the New King James Version®. Copyright © 1982 by Thomas Nelson. Used by permission. All rights reserved.

Scripture marked (KJV) is taken from the King James Version of the Bible. Public domain.

Scripture marked (BSB) is taken from the Holy Bible, Berean Study Bible. Copyright © 2016 by Bible Hub. Used by Permission. All Rights Reserved Worldwide.

Scripture marked (NIV) is taken from the Holy Bible, New International Version®, NIV® Copyright ©1973, 1978, 1984, 2011 by Biblica, Inc.® Used by permission. All rights reserved worldwide.

Scripture marked (DRB) is taken from the Douay-Rheims 1899 American Edition. Public domain.

Scripture marked (NLT) is taken from the Holy Bible, New Living Translation. Copyright © 1996, 2004, 2015 by Tyndale House Foundation. Used by permission of Tyndale House Publishers Inc., Carol Stream, Illinois 60188. All rights reserved.

Scripture marked (NASB) is taken from the New American Standard Bible. Copyright © 1960, 1962, 1963, 1968, 1971, 1972, 1973, 1975, 1977, 1995 by The Lockman Foundation.

Scripture marked (ESV) is taken from the Holy Bible, English Standard Version. Copyright © 2001 by Crossway Bibles, a publishing ministry of Good News Publishers.

Scripture marked (BLB) is taken from the Berean Literal Bible, biblehub.com/blb.

To my wife Nikki, the love of my life—the single greatest reason and reward I can hold;

To my children, Angelina, Nikki, Giuseppe, and Eliana, who are my joy and inspiration;

To my team, who is my family in blood and trial: Mom and Dad, Javen and Caitlin;

To my family; those who were divinely and thoughtfully placed by God to encourage and sharpen me: my Dad, Mom, Chris, Mish, Christine, Joshua, and Kenny and Meagen;

To Mike and Anna, and their beautiful children; those with whom I am learning covenant and communion before our Lord…

…It is to each of you I dedicate this, the cry of my heart.

Contents

Acknowledgments ix
Prologue xi
Greetings xiii

Part 1
The Law

Chapter 1   Via Dolorosa 21
Chapter 2   The (After) Birth 49

Part 2
The Gospels

Chapter 3   The (Bloody) Gospel 71
Chapter 4   Sonship and Circumcision 101
Chapter 5   Brokenness 131

Part 3
The Acts

Chapter 6   Abundant Life 163
Chapter 7   Living Stones 185

Epilogue 207

Acknowledgments

I am compelled to offer thanks to those who have made a way and poured themselves out in love for this project. Also for those who have helped to make me the man who could write this: Tim Beck, Frank Summers, Janet Hart, Michael Dow, and Lenny Maglione; Charles and Christine Donley, Grandpa Sal and Grandma Judy, and David and Nellie Garcia; David A. Knapp and Jack King; Christine Szesnat.

Prologue

Our journey together begins with a most famous verse of Scripture, written by David, the psalmist, whose heart God adored:

> The Lord is my shepherd;
> I shall not want.
> He makes me to lie down in green pastures;
> He leads me beside the still waters.
> He restores my soul;
> He leads me in the paths of righteousness
> For His name's sake.
>
> Yea, though I walk through the valley
> of the shadow of death,
> I will fear no evil;
> For You are with me;
> Your rod and Your staff,
> they comfort me.
>
> You prepare a table before me
> in the presence of my enemies;
> You anoint my head with oil;
> My cup runs over.
> Surely goodness and mercy shall follow me
> all the days of my life;
> And I will dwell in the house of the Lord
> Forever.

—Psalm 23

Greetings...

*J*esus of Nazareth, our Christ and the Savior of the world, was scourged before being hanged to die on a Roman cross. He rose again.

Judas Iscariot, never knowing the resurrection, hanged from a tree by his own device, and was dashed onto the rocks below after falling from a broken rope.

John, the beloved, is the only of the original twelve disciples supposed to have died naturally. After ministering from Jerusalem into Asia Minor, John served the church at Ephesus and cared for Mary, Jesus's mother. After being boiled in oil and surviving, he was exiled to Patmos where he was given the Revelation of the Christ and eventually died.

James, the son of Zebedee, was the first of the original Twelve to die for Christ. He was executed by Herod in 44 AD.

James, the son of Alphaeus, ministered in what is now modern-day Syria. He is said to have survived being thrown from the pinnacle of the temple, only then to be clubbed to death.

Andrew found himself declaring the Gospel up into parts of what would become Russia and her satellites: Asia Minor, Turkey, and Greece. It is believed he was crucified.

Thomas carried the Gospel to Eastern Syria and even into India. It has been said that Thomas brought several hundred people to know Jesus during the exhibition of his execution.

Philip took testimony of the Christ and His power into Carthage, North Africa, and Asia Minor. He is said to have *brought a Roman consulate's wife into relationship with Christ. He was eventually arrested and executed.*

Matthew went to Persia and Ethiopia. He is believed to have been stabbed to death there for preaching Christ.

Bartholomew travelled to India, Armenia, Ethiopia, and Saudi Arabia ministering the Gospel and was eventually martyred.

Simon the Zealot refused to worship the false sun god in Persia where he was testifying to the Christ and was killed for it.

Judas, also known as Thaddeus, preached Jesus to pagans in Mesopotamia where historians say he was beaten to death with sticks.

Matthias, who replaced Judas Iscariot, was burned at the stake after bringing the Gospel into parts of Syria.

Peter was put to death in Rome. Not believing himself worthy of the same death as Jesus, he was nailed to a cross upside down at his own request. This was all after having led Jews in the way of Christ throughout the Roman Empire.

Paul, though not an original disciple, was the single most influential minister of the Gospel to the Gentile world. He followed Christ in breaking the traditions which excluded people outside of Jewish heritage from knowing God. Paul travelled extensively preaching the Gospel and oversaw many early churches, and his letters comprise the majority of New Testament canon. After spending years awaiting the day the Lord would allow him to preach the Gospel in the Roman capital, he was beheaded there for that very act, some say on the same day Peter was crucified.

All of these followed in the footsteps of John the Baptizer, the first to declare the coming Kingdom of heaven and the one appointed by the Father to baptize the Son. John was beheaded in 27 or 28 AD at the request of King Herod's stepdaughter and his wife on the king's birthday. His head was presented to the girl as a trophy for a dance that pleased the king.

None of these men were accountable to denominational[1] leadership. At the mercy of the sword, they hadn't the luxury of choosing doctrines to define their relationships. They served Christ, each other, and the lost; *no matter the cost.*

I do not believe they saw their work in light of dispensationalism,[2] yet I am fairly certain they lived in tribulation. There is no record of them ever preaching about rapture. They preached Jesus, revealed Jesus, and nothing more.

There is no history which outlines how often, and even if, the apostles who built the Church ever voluntarily prayed in tongues *as we know it*. Surprisingly, none of them saw fit to clarify this. Only Paul felt the need to exhort believers to submit this gift and all the others to the Spirit and the believers, so that they be used for the sole purpose of edifying the Body and glorifying the Son. Their faith and power came from knowing Christ and declaring Him, not any person's demonstration of gifts.

Not one of them served in government or endorsed political leaders. They were ambassadors for Christ in a time of open war on those known as followers of *the Way*.[3]

They were never noted for taking a vote. However, they did draw straws and trust the Lord with the fallout.

---

[1] Est. over 34,000 Christian denominations; Status of Global Missions, Gordon-Conwell, 2014.
[2] Dispensationalism is a theological viewpoint which divides God's interactions with mankind into ages, forming boundaries around what He has done, is doing, and will do, based on time periods. One foundation of this belief system focuses on the "rapture" of the Church before an "age" of tribulation that precedes Christ's second coming.
[3] "The Way" is a term that was used to identify the earliest Christians.

After the ascension of Christ, moral failure wasn't attributed to any of these men, and none of them primarily preached morality. Their letters pointed to life in the Spirit and holiness as part of a relationship with Jesus that led them into accountability with each other and to the Lord.

Apparently none of them knew how to name and claim prosperity.

I'm sure they didn't have access to any bottled miracle water.

They never had the privilege of sending prayer requests, along with a check, to any "anointed" televangelist.

They must not have read the prayer of Jabez on the way to any of their *crosses*...

> *Oh, that you would bless me and enlarge my territory!*
> *Let your hand be with me, and keep me from harm*
> *so that I may be free from pain.*[4]

The biblical and historical evidence suggests, at least by current Christian standards, that our best life now was not intended for their lives then, even though I would venture to say their lives were indeed driven by a purpose. I, for one, cannot but drift into thoughts of those who lived for Christ throughout the past ages of persecution, or for the ones who paid with their lives for the Chinese church through her years of agonizing growth to near 100 million strong;[5] for those interned in North Korean camps for professing

---

[4] See 1 Chronicles 4:10 for the biblical text. This prayer is a revelation of God's grace. However, it is not a platform to build any doctrines suggesting we can pray our way out of the humility of a life walking as Christ did.

[5] Taken from an article in *The Washington Post*, headlined, "Christians in China feel full force of authorities' repression," 12/23/2015.

Christ, or for the thousands being cleansed out of Iraq and Syria under the current terror of a rising caliph....

All that the men and women of the early church knew was Jesus.[6] It was the same for those who walked with and followed them. Christ's life was real in them and they demonstrated it in word, power, and deed, everywhere they went. They lived in unity and joy, despite at times disagreeing.

Their union was by the Spirit of Christ and their joy was in fellowship with the living Christ Himself. Not just in one of them; not only one sect or division of believers. Christ was alive in the communion of the saints who were bonded in trial and persecution, and sanctified from the world that wanted them dead or—at the very least—domesticated. Everything they were, and did, was resolved under one driving theme: Jesus Glorified.

These were the marked ones who practiced the discipleship Jesus Himself defined. These were ones willing to pay with blood in order that they might receive only Jesus as their reward. They sought not success, influence, or power—yet gained them all by every one of God's measures because experiencing Jesus was sweeter to them than any temporary thing.

The temptation here is to brush their call aside. For many of us, looking back to the disciples is like watching "special" people who have a superior call or some extraordinary circumstances through which God can meet them differently than those of us who are normal. But I ask you to listen closely. I ask you to open your heart to the voice of the Spirit that calls out *"deeper"* to us all. You don't need anything more than Jesus to answer His call. Your family, your nine-to-five job, and any other thing you see as a limitation is not beyond God's ability to take hold of your life.

---

[6] Suggested reading: *Revolution*, by Gene Edwards.

Come to Jesus. Come as you are. Come from whatever place He has called you. *Just come.*

I am alive to be a burning one that will walk the one bloody road to glory. Together, with some of the burning ones I have been privileged to stand with in this life, let us walk this journey together by light of the One Eternal Flame....

PART 1

THE LAW

"OUR CONDITION."

1

Via Dolorosa

> What kind of a God is He who would choose crucifixion
> as the deepest statement of His nature?
> —*Art Katz, And They Crucified Him*[7]

Our journey begins on a Judean hillside where Jesus the Nazarene is speaking to a crowd. Gathered around this man are a group of disciples and some who have come out from the nearest village. Jesus is on a preaching and teaching tour through the cities and towns from which His disciples originated. Along for the ride are a growing number of stragglers who have been watching the momentum of His miracles and bold statements gain steam at a pace most Jews could only dream about. Jewish hope for the coming messiah was long mixed into the foundations of the Hebrew nation. But these are now a people oppressed by the rule of an unholy Roman Empire.

The Jews were long ago called to be God's representative people on the earth, and they are instead forced to submit the faith of their forefathers to the government of pagan gentiles. They live daily by the agenda of Rome; their food is rationed, they have no army or national defense, and their justice system is closely monitored by

---

[7] Art Katz, *And They Crucified Him* (Bemidji, MN: Burning Bush Press, 2011), Kindle edition.

Rome's proxies. Make no mistake, Jesus is making waves as a potential messiah and everyone wants to see if this is really the deliverer they've been waiting for.

On this day, a steady procession of sick and disenfranchised villagers is causing the crowd size to slowly grow as they come out to see the man some are calling *the One*. The air is thick with expectation. Many have come before this Jesus, claiming to be "the one" Israel has been waiting for since the moment God called her a nation out of Jacob's lineage. Standing there, in that crowd, you can feel the electricity. The tension is time-hardened skepticism colliding with the words of a man who's been setting Judean hillsides like this on fire.

> **Jesus is making waves as a potential messiah and everyone wants to see if this is really the deliverer they've been waiting for.**

The closer you draw to the people in the center of the crowd—the ones who had seen Him cast the demon out of the mute and those who were there when He raised the dead girl up—the more you feel in your heart that something is different this time. It's the unyielding way He moves as a man with nothing to prove, while standing immovable in every statement He makes. It's like nothing you've ever seen before.

It doesn't take long for you to realize, along with most of those around you pressing in for a first look at the Nazarene, that you're in for a confusing surprise. *This is the Messiah?* You've heard He was from Nazareth, but this can't be real. This "messiah" couldn't possibly be preparing to overthrow the Romans and restore the throne of David. You think, almost out loud, *This is definitely a sham. These guys are gonna get what's coming to them.*...

Then, a shout from the preacher draws you back to the center of the throng, "What did you go out into the wilderness to see? A reed shaken by the wind?"[8]

It takes you a moment to understand what He is saying. *What a ridiculous question. I came out to see the miracles! "A reed shaken by the wind?"* you hear repeated in your head. *Who would come all the way out here just to see the wind blowing some brush? This is the same old nonsense. We see enough preachers and their antics at the temple.* By now you are murmuring your frustration out loud. Overhearing you grumble, the guy next to you points to a few men in the distance who are headed for Jerusalem.

As he struggles to keep Jesus in view and fights not to miss any of His words, the man quickly tells you the small group he pointed to was a few of John the Baptizer's followers. He said they had just asked Jesus if He was the coming One or if they should expect another.[9] The man then smiles a bit and cracks that he's glad he didn't sacrifice his reputation for the crazy desert prophet. "Herod has John in prison," he tells you. "You know how that goes. John must be second-guessing his ministry a little."

"Well what did Jesus tell John's men?" you ask.

Still jockeying for position, the man answers you, his breath a little more rushed this time, "He told them to go back to tell John all the miracles they've been seeing. He mentioned healing the blind and lepers. He even said something about the dead coming alive. Apparently they've seen more too, and they've been following Jesus and His disciples for a while."

Quickly you both turn back as Jesus is shouting again, this time a slight sarcasm lacing His voice. "But what did you go out to see? A man dressed in soft clothing? Only

---

[8] Adapted from the events surrounding the gospel of John, chapter 11.
[9] Suggested reading: *The Prisoner in the Third Cell* by Gene Edwards.

the rich rulers wear rich men's clothes. And rich rulers are found in kings' houses."

Now it's becoming clear that Jesus is speaking to you. He's speaking to that man next to you too. He's speaking to all the others here that are just like you. Sarcastically you think a response to His words, *Yeah Jesus, forgive us for expecting our "Messiah" to look like Israel's king....*

Standing before you is a man who just challenged everything Israel has wanted to believe about their Messiah.

As if responding to your thought, Jesus sternly asks, "What did you go all the way out there to see? A *prophet*!" He shouts. Then, in one swift, determined motion, Jesus turns and points in the direction of John's followers, now a good distance off. "Yes! And even more than a prophet! For this is the one who was written about...."

It is at this moment it all begins to come together. Standing before you is a man who just challenged everything Israel has wanted to believe about their Messiah. He has stripped the ancient calling of all of its prestige and fame. Make no mistake, this guy isn't only claiming to be the coming One; He is totally recalibrating the terms of the covenant with Yahweh[10] as your people have desired to see it fulfilled. To this common Jew, like so many others, the changes don't look all that appealing.

AN ISSUE OF BLOOD

Some distance away, John the Baptizer is being held in a prison by Herod. The man who spent most of his life in

---

[10] Yahweh is the written word derived from its sound for the Hebrew name of God, to Jews considered unspeakable and unable to be written.

the desert wearing camel hair and eating locust and honey was now wasting away in a dank stone cell. His share of the Messiah's coming doesn't seem to be paying out very well.

John had lived a life set apart unto the Lord. He had consecrated himself, obeyed, and stayed within the call and sending of the Holy Spirit. John was noted for a life of devotion to the Lord. His disciples acknowledged as much when they said to Jesus, "John came fasting,"[11] inquiring of Jesus's own commitment to God in light of the price they watched John pay.

John gave himself utterly unto the Lord and the Lord spoke through John to declare the coming of the Christ. Jesus Himself would affirm, "…among those born of women there has not risen one greater than John." Of course, the validity of all these words hinged on whether or not Jesus actually was who He said He was. And it is there we find ourselves back in that crowd, face-to-face with what Jesus had to say.

You think to yourself, *John is the greatest? Did He just say that? Does Jesus not know of Abraham, or Moses; of David or Elijah? His own followers just left here asking if Jesus was the real messiah. John's in prison.* Now the thoughts are running faster than you can process them. *That's the way friends of this messiah end up? I can't really believe this…can I? Look at this Jesus anyway, shouting at us, claiming He's the one. He has nothing. I'm even dressed better than He is. What can this carpenter do for Israel?*

Right about now it is becoming apparent that today's show isn't going to be all about signs and wonders. Some in the crowd seem to be realizing the same thing because it's obvious they're growing impatient with all the preaching. The people want action. At this very moment

---

[11] Refer to the events of the gospel of Matthew, chapter 9 for more on this.

Jesus is going on about the pagan cities of Tyre and Sidon and He's comparing His listeners to the wicked people of those places. *I think I've had enough.* And with some of the others, you turn to make your way back into town. There's still many coming out to see Him, but you're pretty sure it won't be long now until this all begins to dissolve.

Jesus knew exactly what He was doing. Every word He chose on the hillside that day was delivered with pinpoint accuracy. When Jesus told John's followers to go back and tell *The Baptizer* everything they saw, Jesus knew they would have to deal with the conflicting realities colliding before them. On the one hand John was the guy those men had staked it all for. They gave up jobs, relationships, reputations, even their lives for John—and he wasn't even being honored at the right hand of this supposed Messiah King. In fact, before John and his followers, the desert prophet wouldn't even be clearly endorsed by Jesus.

> **What they had seen were things only God could perform.**

But on the other hand, what was it exactly that they had seen? Scripture from this account tells us "the blind see, and the lame walk, the lepers are cleansed, and the deaf hear; the dead are raised up and the poor have the Gospel preached to them." What they had seen were things only God could perform.

It is true they didn't see the messiah of their expectations; a man of worldly esteem and power doing what great men do. But for the entire trip to Jerusalem they would have walked, talked, and retold every miracle they had seen—miracles which no man could possibly perform on his own. No king could raise the dead.

What they saw and reported to John could only be the work of God. What they saw was that regardless of where it got him, and even though he himself denied it, John the

Baptizer must have been the prophet who was crying out in the wilderness, "Prepare the way of the Lord...."[12] And that because of one simple fact: this miracle-working Jesus must indeed be the Christ.

As you continue back home, the questions begin to churn in your gut. *Maybe this Jesus is The One after all. Maybe I should go back to Him. But what is the reward for being God's man?* In the midst of a million conflicting emotions, the next thought to cross your mind seems reasonable. *If only John had known when to stop. If only he had stayed with Jesus at the end. Maybe he just missed it and picked one too many fights with Herod. After all, John was human.* But something isn't sitting quite right.

You know some of the guys who said they'd seen Jesus perform miracles. They aren't crazy. And you can't seem to understand why in the world John would go to prison if this Jesus was just a crackpot. It's not like John got anything out of the deal. For that matter, Jesus and none of His guys seem to be getting anything so great out of this either. *So why would anyone even be a disciple of Jesus?*

Your thoughts are rambling as your heart quivers for a moment. *The way He looked at us. Maybe He really believed every word He spoke.* And it was those words He had spoken that wouldn't lay quietly in your chest....

* * *

On that day, on that hillside, Jesus knew exactly where John was headed. And on that day, on that hillside, only Jesus knew that He Himself was, in fact, headed to the very same place. But two thousand years later, having been afforded the luxury of history in knowing what Jesus knew,

---

[12] Mark 1:3

somehow we still find ourselves with many of the same attitudes as those in that crowd.

Somehow, even though we study our Bibles, and even though we sit in plush padded seats with four-dollar coffees and iPhone Bible apps equipped with every biblical translation and commentary, we so easily forget that John's reward for faithful service to Jesus was a brutal beheading at the request of a debased young girl and a lustful king.[13] And somehow, even if we can justify overlooking the price that John paid and chalk it up to the fact that he was an Old Testament prophet, then what exactly do we do with the original twelve disciples?

> **How is it that we can look to the One we claim to follow and be surprised when our path winds up at a cross?**

How many of them died swinging from trees, or nailed to them, or brutalized and bloodied to the point of death in some other savage way? And Jesus Himself? How is it that we can look to the One we claim to follow and be surprised when our path winds up at a cross? Discipleship is, and always was, an issue of blood. And this, my friend, is a book about discipleship.

ROSE-COLORED GLASSES

Anything seen from the wrong perspective winds up looking distorted. Put on the wrong set of glasses and suddenly things which are perfectly fine appear twisted or broken. The eyes are fine and the object is fine but the perspective between them is out of whack. It's just like the

---

[13] Refer to the gospel of Mark, chapter 6, for the complete account of John's death.

morning glare of a sunny day as you're driving to work. It makes everything difficult to see. *For now we see through a glass, darkly.*[14]

When I was a teenager I had run from the Lord and hard into the arms of the world. Drugs, loneliness, and fear created the space for sin to rule my life. I took up a position of defiance before the Lord. I came into the church young; I knew its movements, its language, and how to play the part. For that very reason it was easy to criticize. But honestly I didn't want there to be anything right with the church because then I'd have no excuse to justify myself and my separation.

I make this point because, as I make my next, I want to be very careful. There really is no way for me to view "God's Church" completely unbiased. I have a history with the Church. I am a part of the Church. I am in love with Jesus, and the Church is His bride. Criticizing the Church is the first sign that I am not qualified to do so. This is so important. It is very easy to begin an inventory of ourselves, or the condition of something we are closely attached to, with good intentions. But good intentions just aren't good enough.

David Wilkerson, the beloved founding pastor of Times Square Church, used to preach, "The road to hell is paved with good intentions." If we venture down the path of self and church evaluation, we must do it without attempting to interpret the hearts of men, unless it is our own. When we find ourselves so judging internally, we should never voice our criticism of others for fear of having the spotlight find its focus on our own hypocrisies. We must learn to view everything as Jesus did, with the eyes of the Spirit.

---

[14] 1 Corinthians 13:12 (KJV)

With that understood, I lay this before you: You will be hard-pressed to find true disciples of Jesus in this day. Though there are many great plans out there for manufacturing them, and though there are great resources being poured out around the globe to invest in them, and though there are incredibly healthy (meaning fat, more than resilient) networks built by generations of world missions and church-planting initiatives, there is a clear lack of Christ-possessed men and women around the world corporately displaying His love and nature. There most certainly is a dearth of men and women in the institutional church committed to bearing the image of Christ *regardless of the platform they've been given*—or "lack" thereof.

The bar has been set in the shape of a "T" for those who might choose to walk as disciples of Christ. A disciple bears the one undeniable weight of Christ in their life: a bloody cross. A disciple may not know the language, may not have perfected the movements of popular Christian culture, and might not hold the cleanest theological positions. A disciple, depending on where you find them in their journey, might not yet look very much like Jesus in outward expression. But in the life of a follower of the Christ you will find one who has, at the very least, turned from the way of the world, who has been shown by the Spirit the insatiable hunger of their own flesh, and has submitted themselves to the light of God.

Jesus said in John's gospel[15] that men reject Jesus because they do not want their sin to be exposed. Anyone, at any point, who is willing to be purified by the truth and light of Jesus and lays their life down completely to the process of the Lord, is His disciple. This will look like something. No disciple is without change. But we often get sidetracked by comparing different people's paths and pace

---

[15] See John 3:20,21.

of change which are only developed by the Spirit Himself. He leads each of us according to grace and our ability to respond. **Faith, *if it has no works, is dead.*** [16]

A disciple is one who has turned from the world, exposed themselves to Christ while learning to continually behold Him, and is being transformed while following Jesus in a life of Spirit-initiated action. Over time, and through intimacy with Jesus, the outward expression of a disciple will become more like that of Jesus Himself. You cannot stay near Him and *not* be changed. And it is through this process that disciples are forged into the brick and mortar which form the corporate Body of Christ; the fellowship, brotherhood, or communion of men and women who *together*, bear the image and glory of Christ upon the earth.

> **You cannot stay near Him and not be changed.**

Christianity for the most part, both personally and in the expression of the organized church, has grown into a sort of uber-fraternity that seeks the blessings of God, personal growth, political, and social influence. We want a form of godliness,[17] rather than God Himself, and we want a moral framework to justify our self-indulgence. Even though God's Word has laid out for us what is to come, and Jesus's life reveals to us the posture we should take in the face of the world's demands, we still tend toward a reality that is lower than God's design for us. This is not a new occurrence in the relationship between God and man. We have a selfish flaw in us that tends to take what God is doing and somehow interpret it for our own personal well-being, rather than being able to see the liberty and

---

[16] James 2:17

[17] See 2 Timothy 3 for Paul's warning against those having "a form of godliness."

life presented to us in detaching from a life pointed at self-gratification.

When we muddy the waters with religious speak and action, yet aren't actually being transformed by closeness to Jesus, things get even harder to see because everything around us encourages us to keep going based on external results. We might live well, or be good and act "Christian," but still be an inwardly twisted mess of selfish motives and hidden offense that only God can see. And regardless of how we spin what we do as "so we can bless others" and "for the benefit of the Church or the lost," it's really just a self-preserving human bend toward blindness, particularly in the areas that we know will be painful or cost us more than we want to pay for true change.

Let's take a walk on the road to Emmaus to briefly illustrate this point. In chapter 24 of Luke's gospel, verses 13-27 tell the story of two of Jesus's disciples walking to a town called Emmaus. The timing is a few short days after Jesus was crucified. The stories of Him appearing were beginning to circulate among the believers. This was little solace for the ones who had basically left their lives, surrendered their reputations, and gambled everything they ever dreamt of becoming on the fact that Jesus was going to be their deliverer and the man who'd lead the Jews back to world prominence.

As the story unfolds, we read that they were walking along and talking of the things that had happened in Jerusalem—namely that Jesus was just put to death. The Scripture tells us that Jesus appears beside them (the first clue He might be different) but they could not recognize Him. Some translations say their eyes were "restrained" while other describe it like "they were kept from seeing Him." Then, in verse 17, He asks them something like, "What are you talking about that is making you so sad?"

It is remarkable to me that men who followed Jesus for almost three years—men who listened to Him, walked by Him, ate with Him, and I am sure once in a while took a bath next to Him in a river—could somehow be blind to who He was. And this goes on for a while. If you read the biblical account, you see that Jesus talks to them about Himself and even goes through the Law and the Prophets (the Jewish Bible) to explain how the things which transpired in Jerusalem were the exact events God ordered for the Messiah.

So the question is, for these Jewish men who'd been raised in religious ways and had even seen the Gospel unfold before them, what were they missing? Well, to start, they were missing *real faith* in the right things. It is obvious if you read that these guys were struggling to believe eternal things over what they had physically witnessed. At this point, Jesus's death was way more real to them than His resurrection. Their faith was aligned with the results their expectations created, rather than being anchored in who Jesus was.

Second, they were missing the life of the Spirit in their hearts. The Teacher, as Holy Spirit is described in Scripture, was not being clearly heard. And if He was, they were not connected to Him deeply enough to understand. I believe Holy Spirit was still an external being, as was Jesus walking beside them that day. Jesus had not yet breathed on the disciples, filling them with His Spirit.[18] However, the point that I want to spend a minute on here refers more to what it was that they expected to see in Jerusalem a few days earlier.

Remember, Jesus explained God's Word to them in relation to the prophets in order that they would see that it was actually God's plan for Jesus to bleed on a Roman

---

[18] The gospel of John 20:22

cross. Can you see how these men imposed their own expectations into their hope for a different outcome? Even after those earlier days on the hillsides of Judea, and after Jesus pointed to the Baptizer's example of sacrifice and death as the highest honor in service to God; after three years of validating His own words with signs and wonders and then fulfilling the Law and prophecies as no man in history, crucifixion was simply not in their plans. ***Set your minds on things that are above.***[19]

Jesus knew exactly what He was saying when He uttered the words, "Whoever wants to be My disciple must deny themselves and take up their cross and follow Me. For whoever wants to save their life will lose it, but whoever loses their life for Me will find it." Is there anything stronger in all the created world than the human will to survive?

We avoid death with every action we choose, and even the involuntary ones are all designed to keep us alive. We pay for longer life, and we spend our lives working to make them bigger, better, and more satisfying in every way we know how. But what if there is more to satisfaction than we can possibly extract from the temporal things in this life? What if Jesus's words were true and He understood something about us that began under a tree in Eden, exalted itself on a tower at Babel, refused to climb the mountain at Sinai, wouldn't pay the Baptizer's price, and finally failed to see the answer hanging from Calvary's bloody crossbeam?

You see, the point I am trying to get to is that not every churchgoer is a disciple of Jesus. A student of the Bible is not a disciple of Jesus, though Jesus's disciples most likely study His Word. A ministry leader is not a disciple of Jesus, though some of Jesus's disciples do lead ministries. A miracle worker isn't a disciple of Jesus, though there is little doubt that disciples of Jesus work miracles in the earth.

---

[19] Colossians 3:2 (ESV)

A disciple of Jesus is a man or woman who has picked up their cross and followed Him to that brutally bloody place of exhibition, whereby they can be lifted in moments of humiliation as living sacrifices for their brethren and before their Father. A disciple of Jesus is not one who seeks to learn Christianity as a culture and find ways to advance within the religious system of growth in gifting and ministry skill, *even if* it is in order to fulfill the "great commission."[20] A disciple of Jesus is one that is willing to forego every possible promise of what might appear to be a blessing in this momentary life and give up everything in pursuit of the One True God who went to a cross to bleed out so that we could eternally live.

> **A disciple of Jesus is a man or woman who has picked up their cross and followed Him to that brutally bloody place of exhibition.**

So who are the disciples that you know? Now before you list every Christian that you love, or who has done amazing things *for* Jesus—even those whose lives seem to be blessed with favor and prosperity—make sure you understand the question. Who is it that you know who is ready and willing to leave everything in the blink of an eye simply because the word of the Lord came to them and asked them to do so?

Who are the people you know that would even leave the safety of the church they've been a part of since birth, or pastoring for eleven years now, to follow Jesus—if *He* led them into a wilderness season? And I don't mean a seven-day testing of the Lord to not watch TV or eat ice cream. I mean the wilderness of stripping, where everything in life

---

[20] See the gospel of Matthew 28:16-20.

is on the table and Jesus might actually require your "Isaac" to be slaughtered rather than spared.[21]

Who are the people you see that when I ask you if they were promised to be rejected, not only by the world, but by the Church, would still obey the Lord without a doubt? If you are like most of us, your list is very short. Maybe enough to count with the fingers of one hand. Maybe, if you've been blessed with a special grace in your life, you'd be using fingers from both hands. You would certainly be the exception.

You have to see past the outward success. Look beyond the hype and praise of men. Don't pay attention to the size of a person's gift. Disciples of Jesus all have one thing in common. Disciples of Jesus are all covered in blood, because all of Jesus's disciples have submitted themselves to the life of the cross. ***Let us fix our eyes on Jesus...who for the joy that was set before Him endured the cross.***[22]

It goes back to that matter of perspective, really. Remember that hillside again. Do you remember what it was like being a first-century Jew that day and listening to Jesus speak? Do you remember what it was like to carry expectations of the Messiah built on years of teaching from the rabbis and temple leaders to go along with the generations of family and national tradition? How all of these dynamics collided fueling the hope that somehow your people would be respected and honored among the nations again? Can you remember the feelings of pressure that you had to live up to the hype, displaying for the Messiah a righteousness that He might reward, or at the very least recognize, when He finally got the privilege of encountering *you?*

---

[21] Refer to the events of Genesis, chapter 22, and the commentary of this event in the Letter to the Hebrews, chapter 11:17-19.
[22] Hebrews 12:2 (BLB)

Of course you and I cannot really remember those emotions. We are not first-century Jews. But we certainly can try to comprehend for a second what those emotions were when Jesus began to point toward Herod's dungeon, soon to be upgraded for an execution stage. I'm sure you can imagine what it felt like as Jesus alluded to His very own crucifixion which would soon follow. Maybe a little fear? Arrogance? Maybe just a little resistance?

> **In our day, there is rarely a man or woman who calls people to the cross.**

As those emotions set in there would be one of those troubling, lingering questions sitting in your soul. The kind which, at least for a second, makes you question everything your world is built on. Now that you know better, and since we have the luxury of Scripture as a historical guide, imagine how you might have felt if you actually knew then the outcome Jesus was pointing to was the humiliation and pain of a cross.

I am thankful for the grace of a God who pours out His love and, in at least some measure I can understand, reveals Himself so that the call to the cross can be seen for what it is: a price worth paying for a reward which we as sinners should never even get the chance to taste. I am drawn to the words of Simon Peter as he answered the Christ's question in the face of so many who had departed grasping the reality of the call, "'Do you also want to go away?' But Simon Peter answered Him, 'Lord, to whom shall we go? You have the words of eternal life...You are the Christ, the Son of the living God.'"[23]

In our day, there is rarely a man or woman who calls people to the cross. Hardly a preacher can be found who

---

[23] John 6:67-69

points to the cross as the cost of entrance into the Kingdom. Rarer is the one who willingly picks up his own cross to follow Jesus. In fact, we have crafted doctrines, fashioned wholesale evangelism crusades, and built entire denominational movements on the premise that coming to Jesus will be the answer to temporal, earthly problems. We tell people that the grace Jesus has freely made available to us means walking with Jesus will cost us nothing. Never has humanity been sold a more fraudulent bill of goods.

Think about this. Someone is sick? Come to Jesus and you'll receive healing. Who is struggling financially? Jesus is your source and provider! Does anyone have a broken marriage? If you come to Jesus, He will fix your broken marriage. For the most part the rewards of encountering Jesus are dangled as proverbial carrots from a preacher's stick, advertisements of sorts as to why we should come to the front for the minister to touch us, call the 1-800 number, or put a check in the envelope so our prayers can get answered. Even when it's not a "ministry" dangling the carrot, many of us have learned to preach the same way to our friends and loved ones.

Now understand, there are many angles to this conversation. But let's really consider this. Yes, Jesus is our healer! Yes, Jesus is our provider! Thankfully, He is able to restore a broken marriage and provide an answer for the most desperate crisis. However, these alone are not the reasons for submitting your entire life to Him. When someone you love beats breast cancer, do they suddenly leave everything and follow the doctor? What if someone bailed you out financially? Would you leave everything and everyone, join their club, and begin calling them Mom or Dad? And what about the therapist or marriage counselor that helped spare us from a recent family crisis? Would that be grounds for us to suddenly allow them to have influence in every area of our lives and begin referring to their friends and followers as brother and sister so-and-so?

No, the thought is actually getting more ridiculous to me as I write it. But this is the way many, if not most, are introduced to man's version of the Kingdom of heaven. It's exactly what most people hear when they are brought into a church. In light of these shenanigans, we all-knowing Christians still bicker over whether or not to expose our children to Santa Claus and the tooth fairy!

> **When we learn to fully trust Him it means we are finally about to fly.**

Jesus railed at those who followed Him simply because of miracles and used faith as a means to gain earthly reward. He called them "blind"[24] and "thieves."[25] He pointed out their hypocrisy. He relentlessly called them out because He knew that the empty human craving for signs would never be satisfied without the vulnerable closeness of a relationship with Him.

An approach to God too focused on sensual satisfaction only breeds a lust for His benefits in the place of His affection, and eventually devolves into a constant need for Him to prove that He's still even there. This is the antithesis of what it is to be a child—to live in the unblemished freedom of a reality that your daddy loves you and will always be there. There are times Daddy puts you on His lap to take you for a ride and times He lets go of the handlebars so you can figure out how to stay upright on your own. When we learn to fully trust Him it means we are finally about to fly.

Look, the parts of God found in Jesus which are miraculous are many. His ability to do anything and everything

---

[24] Matthew 15:14
[25] John 10:8-10

is, in itself, a proof of who God is. They are beautiful parts of Himself by which He desires to be revealed and He longs for us to come to know Him. He wants to be your healer, provider, guide, fortress, counselor, hope, and so much more. But to be a disciple of His, Jesus never beckoned anyone by way of these partial expressions of Himself. He called to something so much deeper than just our sensual and emotional experiences.

Jesus looked at those twelve men, and hillsides of others as well, and He invited them to follow something so much greater than they had ever seen. He invited them into the promise of life eternal through the act of crucifixion. I want to say with a clear and resounding "YES!" that this did include the experience of His miraculous life and glory, even while they walked with Him in the earth.

But make no mistake, the call to the Gospel of Jesus Christ is a call to join Him in death and suffering.

Paul wrote to the Colossian church, "For you have died, and your life is hidden with Christ in God. When Christ who is your life appears, then you also will appear with Him in glory."[26] Until you've tasted His goodness, it is hard to see such things as more than punishment for human flaws which we seem to have no control over. But the call to the cross is the death that liberates us from ourselves. It is the crucifixion of self-glorification, self-trust, self-reliance, and anything in us which exalts what this world has to offer over the eternally selfless foundations of the Kingdom of heaven.

In fact, this one bloody road is the only way we can ever draw closer to Jesus. This one bloody road is the only place where we will never walk alone and where we will be transformed to partake in the Lord's life, as we witness Jesus do incredible and miraculous things. This one bloody

---

[26] Colossians 3:3,4 (ESV)

road is the same road Jesus walked, and where we begin to understand His glory by laying down as living sacrifices for others, just as He did. The only question is, and has always been, will you come? *He who did not spare His own Son, but delivered Him up for us all, how shall He not with Him also freely give us all things?*[27]

BLOOD-COLORED GLASSES

I think it is very important that a few things get touched on here. The enemy, and our own self-loathing human nature, will use any opportunity available to hijack our walk with the Lord and set us on the wrong course. I have already addressed the human tendency and the condition of comfortable mainstream Christianity to gloss over the walk of discipleship or to pervert it into something that comes with the promise of worldly gain, especially in the name of ministry. But there are countless other ways believers resist truly "losing their life for Me,"[28] as Jesus said.

Some resist the crucified life of discipleship by viewing it as an unattainable reality for the "average person," and therefore futile to pursue. Others will go to extremes in trying to create places of suffering, spiritually camping out as victims, or holding on to some form of holier-than-thou false image of themselves that makes them more deserving of the glory which Jesus reveals through His disciples. The Holy Spirit is the Spirit of grace and truth. It is understanding grace and being anchored in truth which burn away spiritual haze and allow us to clearly see the road to glory passes only through the very life of Christ.

---

[27] Romans 8:32
[28] Luke 9:24

Grace[29] shatters the notion that true discipleship, which journeys through suffering and offers no glory in this life higher than the heavenly privilege of walking with Jesus, is reserved for a select few. Being a part of the corporate bride of Christ isn't something only for those in "ministry" or someone whose life includes a special spiritual privilege.

Every person is infinitely spectacular by design.

Grace means that we have received something we are incapable of attaining or undeserving of having. Grace means that we are entitled to something beyond our own control or design. Grace means the "average person" doesn't even exist because Jesus has made a way for every person to be united to God, and therefore every person is infinitely spectacular by design. Grace means that heaven's definition of normal is not the "status quo" according to earthy standards. According to God's design, a "normal" person is in perfect union with Him. Grace is the perfect picture of this truth and the power behind it on full display. Grace *is* Jesus Himself, *for* Jesus Himself, and given to us.

In other words, when God presented Jesus to us, He was a walking gift of God's goodness and a sign of the eternal disposition of God towards humankind. At the same time that Jesus *was the gift*, He was here *for an eternal purpose*: to die and be raised to life. The *eternal purpose* entitled us to *eternally possess Him*, and be possessed by Him, in the form of His Holy Spirit actually living within us. Jesus's Spirit dwells in all of us who believe in Jesus as

---

[29] Suggested reading on the topic of grace: *Hyper-Grace* by Michael L. Brown.

the Christ *and* follow Him. ***As you received Christ Jesus the Lord, so walk in Him.***[30]

For those who might suggest that actually following Jesus is adding something to Jesus's spoken salvation requirement "to believe," you cannot truly believe in Him and His words and subsequently *not follow Him*. James declared, "I will show you my faith by my works."[31] Jesus said that "those who love Me obey My words."[32] No matter what doctrine you prescribe to, salvation cannot occur aside from loving Christ. Love for Christ is a call to action. Even if you don't want to agree that we must act in order to live out salvation, you cannot possibly protest that the gift of salvation immediately produces action in all who receive it in faith, at least not on any scripturally sound basis. ***But whoever keeps His word, truly the love of God is perfected in him.***[33]

The final thing grace does through the work of the Spirit is to empower us to be transformed into those who live like Jesus in this life—participating with Christ and fellow believers in everything He does in the earth. Whether the most difficult, seemingly unattainable, or even gloriously supernatural things that God does, grace through Christ means we are changed to be like Him while being lifted by the Holy Spirit into doing the very things Jesus does. Grace makes the life of a disciple available to the sinner and transforms us into the sons and daughters of God who bear the image of Jesus in the earth.

> **Love for Christ is a call to action.**

---

[30] Colossians 2:6 (ESV)
[31] James 2:18
[32] See John 14:21-24.
[33] 1 John 2:5

Now, as for those who'd look to add to their own suffering as a means to ascend in spiritual stature, again we turn to grace. Do you remember when Jesus told the disciples that some of them would taste the same death as He did and others would be spared?[34] As our guide, it is up to Holy Spirit to determine when, where, and how we face trials in this life. He chooses the deserts. He calls the harvest forth and chooses who will partake in the reaping. When we add suffering or hold on to suffering beyond what the grace of God has allowed in order to lay claim to a little more blessing, a clearer conscience, or to stand taller in the company of God and other believers, we betray that very grace God gave us.

> **We betray Christ when we mimic parts of His lifestyle while at the same times trying to control pieces of our lives.**

Paul wrote to the Galatian churches that if they added requirements of the law like circumcision (which after Christ fulfilled the law would amount to man-made suffering) then they would be required to fulfill every Jewish law, and that what Christ had done in His death would have not been enough to save us.[35] It is grace that both qualifies us and empowers us to be disciples of Christ.

We betray Christ when we mimic parts of His lifestyle while at the same time trying to control pieces of our lives. He should be leading us through everything. We falsely assume we can earn more of something spiritual by accomplishing plans we concocted. Jesus told Nicodemus that flesh only gives birth to flesh, and spirit only gives birth to

---

[34] See Matthew 16:24-28.
[35] Read Galatians chapters 3-5; I recommend *The Message* translation.

spirit.[36] In other words, we cannot humanly come up with something to do that results in what only the Spirit of God can produce. Only when the Spirit is at work can we do anything that will pass the test of eternity.

No matter how good it sounds or how impressive it looks, we cannot strive, starve, or negotiate ourselves into anything worthy of Jesus. The idea that we can set any of the terms with God is the most fundamentally bankrupt premise one can carry into building a relationship with Him, yet it is found in the foundations of every religious system in the world. ***Beware lest anyone cheat you through philosophy and empty deceit, according to the tradition of men.***[37]

Paired with the grace which Jesus personifies, is truth, of which Jesus is also the perfect embodiment. There is no aspect of our walk, of our lives, or of eternity that Jesus doesn't portray. I love it when I hear Bill Johnson, the senior pastor of Bethel Church in Redding, California say that "Jesus Christ is perfect theology." What we see in Him, how Jesus lived, everything Jesus said, and His relationship to both God and mankind, were all perfect. The Word is interpreted correctly when read and received on the foundation that Jesus Christ is, was, and forever will be.

Think about this for a moment. An infinite God lacking nothing chooses to add to Himself by creating something. The something, all of creation in a general sense, having been formed out of nothing, cannot be God based on the simple fact that it did not exist at some point before. God always was, always is, and always will be. But as the highest expression of Himself, God chooses to do this knowing full well that creation will fall short of Him simply because it isn't His equal. The Father creates us knowing that He will

---

[36] See John 3.
[37] Colossians 2:8

be the One who ultimately pays the steepest price for us to be bonded to Him and exist with Him eternally.

Jesus was the cost the Father paid for this transaction. For this reason, Paul's letter to the Ephesians says that all things will be reconciled in Jesus,[38] brought together under Jesus, to reveal Jesus in the unfolding of God's eternal plan. What Paul is saying is that the eternal Jesus—through whom God has united Himself to His created work—is what everything exists by, for, and through. ***All things were created through Him and for Him.***[39]

Everything that has ever happened and will ever happen will ultimately be a part of Jesus or cease to exist. Jesus Christ is the explanation for life and the universe. He is the Truth. So when we talk about being called to discipleship, being called apart to follow Jesus, the process and the result cannot look like anything else but Jesus and what He did.

Any call to religion that includes things which Christ Himself does not possess, or does things He didn't do, has to be recognized as deception.

Hear me on this. I know we carry flesh and that flesh sometimes stinks. It's been corrupted and carries the rot of sin. It will fall at times. But that gets submitted to the Father, purged by the power of the Spirit, and redeemed through walking it out with Jesus. Any call to religion that includes things which Christ Himself does not possess, or does things He didn't do, has to be recognized as deception. Jesus WILL NOT call anyone to exalt themselves. Jesus WILL NOT call anyone to abuse people. He WILL NOT call anyone to divide a church. Will people be offended by

---

[38] See Paul's letter to the Ephesians, chapter 1:7-10.
[39] Colossians 1:16 (ESV)

a man or woman who walks with Jesus? YES. Will things in and around you be shaken, sifted, and burned? YES. Even unto death you will be despised. ***For our God is a consuming fire.***[40]

But Jesus went silently, as a sheep to the slaughter,[41] to do the work His Father prescribed for Him. Jesus rode a donkey[42] into Jerusalem. Jesus lived a broken, humble, and God-glorifying life. He remained pure through it all. There is no call, no doctrine, and no place in discipleship that makes room for sin, because such was not found in Jesus. Sin is a vile desecration of Jesus's work on the cross.

> **Discipleship is the one bloody road on which Christ alive in us can daily be raised to life and glorified for all the world to see.**

Yet despite all being marred by sin, every person has been created by God to be loved and eternally united to Him, and has been deemed worthy of the blood of Jesus for redemption.

As we submit ourselves to Jesus, grace ultimately and continually makes us worthy and transforms us to live as Christ. Jesus is the standard of truth by which grace, and everything else, functions. Becoming a disciple is choosing to walk the one road by which grace is made available to us and on which truth is found—the bloody road where we are daily crucified. Discipleship is the *one bloody road* on which Christ alive in us can daily be raised to life and glorified for all the world to see.

---

[40] Hebrews 12:29
[41] Isaiah 53:7
[42] Zechariah prophesied in chapter 9 of his book of Jesus coming on a donkey; see John 12:14.

2

The (After) Birth

> ...I pray also for those who will believe in me...
> May they also be in us so that the world may believe that
> you have sent me. I have given them the glory that you
> gave me, that they may be one as we are one—I in them
> and you in me—so that they may be brought to complete
> unity. Then the world will know that you sent me and
> have loved them even as you have loved me.
> —John 17:20-23 (NIV)

The purpose of discipleship is the experiential union of God and man in the earth. It is the proving ground of eternal love, by the crucible of choice. Jesus was that man completely united to God, and discipleship is the avenue by which Jesus's life is recreated in the rest of us. God has desired, as an expression of Himself, that fallen men and women would be able to experience Him and become like Him while living in a broken world. It is the ultimate statement of God's nature that He could take something other than Himself—something less than Himself—and bring that lesser thing up into union with Him.

When a frail human enters the eternal place only God inhabits and is able to remain, it testifies to God's omnipotence. For God to do this through relationship and not as a dictator or some grand master of puppets tells us of His heart as a father and the purity in which His love is selflessly poured out on us.

He has not chosen to force us into a certain relationship with Him. We have not been designed with a default setting to love God more than anything else. What we have been designed with is the space to do so and the free will to manage that space. We have been created with a longing to love and be loved with no strings attached. Not even the internal strings that chain us to our self-serving need to be righteously satisfied when we love with great human effort in the face of profound personal risk.

True love originates in God alone. Love must be experienced, voluntary, and tested. And love, by definition, is not self-serving. **Beloved, if God so loved us, we also ought to love one another.**[43]

The event of salvation occurs when we first respond to God's love. Being "saved" is the accepting and receiving of a new eternal identity which Christ has already provided for us.[44] That new identity entitles us to the heavenly right to take part in a process of adoption[45] into God's family and the experience of God's children. But salvation alone was never the sole call of the Christ to His people in this world. What good is being entitled to union with God without apprehending that very thing?

To love someone and yet be separate, or worse—to be bound to another—would not only be a disappointment, but also be a tragic sentence of death for the soul. Such is the case for a person who claims to believe in the Christ but never commits to the life of discipleship which divorces us from the world and marries us to the Lord. Discipleship is the bloody process of being severed from this world by

---

[43] 1 John 4:11
[44] See John 3 for Jesus's explanation of salvation.
[45] See Ephesians 1:3-6 for more on "adoption" in Christ.

crucifying our own desire to rule in some corner of it, all the while being transformed into the very image of Christ by walking with Him on His terms.

How can we describe discipleship as both bloody and glorious in the same sentence? How is it simultaneously a divorce and a marriage? Only when you catch a glimpse of the prize can you begin to understand. Jesus, and His life of perfect union and intimacy with the Father, released a glory into the earth that "all of creation is groaning for."[46]

> **Christ's union with the Father caused Him to release healing, light, and life into every situation He encountered.**

Christ's union with the Father caused Him to release healing, light, and life into every situation He encountered. As He was innocently despised, accused, beaten, and finally hung on a cross, Jesus displayed only love.

At its toughest, His love refused to compromise with sin, because if He did then those trapped in wickedness would be condemned to death without the possibility of life. In essence, if Jesus failed in being one with God, how could He save and empower us to succeed in that same way? At its lowest, Christ's perfect love bled out, naked and broken in the face of humiliation; crying out for the Father to offer a reprieve to those who hung Him there. A perfect God paid the price for us and still offers forgiveness when we kill Him for it. *For God has not destined us for wrath, but to obtain salvation through our Lord Jesus Christ.*[47]

It's in the seventeenth chapter of John's gospel, highlighted at the beginning of this chapter, that Jesus voices the way for those who would come after Him to be brought

---

[46] See Romans 8:22-24.
[47] 1 Thessalonians 5:9 (ESV)

into the eternal family of God and display that very same love to the world. Jesus's prayer for the disciples, and then for those who would follow them, was that they too would walk in the same union with God as He did, and in doing so corporately experience that union as an eternal spiritual family, living in this world.

A real family cannot be held together by name or DNA alone. In the building of God's family there is a requirement that all of us know Him and the intimate fellowship a real family is designed for. The bonds of true family are forged by having walked together through both trial and triumph.

LIFE WORTH DYING FOR?

It is one thing to talk about history and be inspired. It is easy to hear another person's story and feel emotionally compelled to want the same experience. Even getting caught up in the nostalgia of our own memories brings us only so close to the actual reality of an authentic, current experience. But you have to actually be doing something to taste its full experience. As soon as tasting is over, the exuberance soon fades into the longing for more or something new. Watching an IMAX movie isn't the same as jumping off a mountain in a wingsuit. Telling the story of your wedding day shouldn't bring more joy than experiencing your next victory together.

You see, in order for anything to be worth dying for, in order for us to be willing to lay down everything we have and everything we dream of having, there must be a real and tangible value. Who would consider dying and giving up their future for something of little value? Someone who has nothing to live for might; someone who sees no future. Only a promise for something greater than we have now, or the love of something above our love for ourselves, is worth dying for. A religious reward contains no satisfaction now. There is no current experience worthy of your life whose reward can only be tasted after this life is over. *You have tasted that the Lord is good.*[48]

Think about it; religious perfection is unattainable in this imperfect life. Even for the believer, we have Jesus's own words in the Sermon on the Mount[49] as the reference point for religious failure. Remember when He looked at the religious leaders in Matthew's fifth chapter and said to them that even though they acted perfect according to the law, He knew their hearts were still filled with sin? He called them out for murderous and adulterous thinking as enough to be considered unholy before God.

When the pinnacle of spiritual life is following religious laws of piety, it is clear that beauty is only skin-deep. Below our religiously groomed exteriors, it is simply impossible for the human being to train and discipline themselves free of sin. We cannot ever seem to get the heart right by doing good things. Jealousy, comparing, judging, lusting, and just about every other evil is somehow still in our hearts. For this reason, religion only directs us toward the promise of a reward beyond this life as the sole reason for dedication and service.

Since religion doesn't have the answer for our sin, all it can do is promise us that we will receive a reward after this life is over. We give it our best shot, and to the extent that we succeed in following religious law and doing more good than evil, we believe we are earning God's favor for a later date. We then hope we will be rewarded in a life to come. *But Jesus Christ has offered something better.* Jesus has offered us a relationship with God. The reward of

---

[48] 1 Peter 2:3 (NIV)

[49] Matthew, chapter 5 begins Jesus's first recorded public sermon, widely called "The Sermon on the Mount."

relationship is in its current experience. Jesus offers us the cleansing which religion imitates, and the vulnerable exposure of a relationship to God which religion refuses. ***For the law of the Spirit of life in Christ Jesus has set you free from the law of sin and death.***[50]

The sales pitches just aren't true. In our Christian culture we build around growing in the way of an organized church. People are taught that the answer to their internal struggle and search for purpose in life is how they fit into their local community ministry or parish and how well they follow its doctrine. But the writing is on the wall. Most of the Western world is experiencing the demise of the Church[51] as people tire from trying to live good and look good while their insides are screaming. The song and dance of church routines deprived of actual contact with God simply can't shake off the anchor of condemnation weighing on their souls.

> **There are more people questioning their faith in our churches than in nightclubs.**

We see people leaving in droves. Good Christian families with history in the church are slowly withering as "success" in this Christian culture has produced an entire generation of people who can recite the pastor's ten keys to a happy life but aren't finding real peace, joy, and rest. There are more people questioning their faith in our churches than in nightclubs. And in the nightclubs you are more likely to find people willing and hungry to encounter a radically real God who still works miracles.

---

[50] Romans 8:2 (NASB)

[51] Pew Research Center's 2014 *Religious Landscape Study;* 5 million less Americans claimed religious affiliation than in 2007. Studies have been pointing this way for years.

Mirroring the religious history written since the beginning of man's existence, most of the "Christianized" world has grown lazy in its own prosperity. Nobody seeks out something to die for when life is pretty good. Who really wants to sacrifice their decent life for a radical approach that only promises a future religious reward? It is in desperate situations we find people willing to take desperate measures.

In places where life isn't taken for granted and the world around only offers success in better chances of survival, you will find people willing to bet it all on the promise that they might inherit a future paradise. The rise of radical Islam has put this dynamic front and center for us today. There have been times and places in the world where religious organizations have sold Christianity to people much in the same way.

In my life, there was a time when I had nothing to lose. My family was broken, my father's life had just succumbed to the fury of heroin, and I was also an addict staring death in the face. That point of desperation was the place at which I was willing to mortgage my life for the promise of a pardon from God, the hope of some future salvation, and take my chances with a religious reward. His amazing grace is the only reason I now know something far better: the intimacy of relationship beyond what I ever hoped to receive. ***Behold what manner of charity the Father hath bestowed upon us.***[52]

Oh, how different it is to follow Christ! How much easier it would be to simply die for Him, cash in our chips, and receive our reward...*later*. Unless of course, you still had something to live for—like a career, a family, or even just a dream. In that case, you would likely seek more than an unattainable cause for which to die. It's for this very reason that mere religious ritual ceases to be useful for

---

[52] 1 John 3:1 (DRB)

people who overcome the most primal hardships of life and begin to live for comfort and convenience.

To those who hang their hats on past moments of success, religion usually becomes nothing more than a moral anesthetic. People seeking pleasure and fulfillment will not find it in the tension of unattainable religious piety that doesn't make them happy along the way, doesn't relieve the burden of internal guilt, and doesn't provide them a means to some form of leverage in life when it's all said and done.

That's precisely why the call of a Christian goes far beyond becoming part of a religious system. Following religious laws and then dying for the reward isn't a viable way to heaven according to Jesus. Jesus certainly never told anyone to learn to be a better Jew in order to find salvation. Jesus never invited His disciples to march to Golgotha[53] with Him, die, and be immediately transferred to heaven, sins forgiven and crowns mounted on their heads. No, in following Christ, the disciples were invited to pick up their own crosses and to follow Him.

In following Christ, *we* are invited to bear a cross, every day of our lives, and to take it with us wherever Jesus leads us to go. In following Christ, we aren't invited to simply die and receive our promise in one momentary transaction. Jesus said "pick up your cross, and follow Me." These words speak of the continual bearing or carrying of crucifixion. They foretell of a cross that is perpetually part of the journey.

---

[53] Also named Calvary, this was a hill outside of the walls of Jerusalem where people were crucified.

DEATH WORTH LIVING FOR!

Paul described the call of a Jesus follower by saying that "to die *is gain*."[54] Did you catch that? It is the actual process of dying itself that Paul says is the gain. Dying is the process by which life is removed from something. In following Christ, the life of sin and eternal bondage is actually coming out of us as we willfully remain attached to our cross. What does this mean? It means that as we surrender to the dying of our "selves" in giving our life to Jesus, we gain His purity. We gain His innocence before the Father. We gain the freedom of living from the eternal strength that now permanently resides in us by way of God's own Spirit having been restored to us. Dying to ourselves means surrendering our will, our wants, and needs—all of which create expectations based on how we hope things turn out for us—to the process of being crucified on behalf of the life of another.

As we walk through a relationship with the Lord, willing to be broken as He was broken, for the healing of others who may even reject us, we receive the reward of cleansing that allows us to then carry and share God's glory in this life. It is a beautiful paradox, to be at the same time dying in the flesh (referring to our body and will) and living in the Spirit. In Jesus's words, "If anyone desires to come after Me, let him deny himself, and take up his cross, and follow Me. For whoever desires to save his life will lose it, but whoever loses his life for My sake will find it."[55]

How can we be constantly dying if salvation, which is what we obtain when we turn away from sin and follow Jesus, occurs the moment we become children of God and receive eternal life? Shouldn't the dying end? Shouldn't we

---

[54] Philippians 1:21
[55] Matthew 16:24,25

be able to have life *and live* in victory? Well, that answer is...Yes! We live victoriously *as* we are continuously dying on a cross. It is only because we live in the death of continuous surrender that we can be forever found in the place of Christ's resurrection. Such a life is constantly poised for a glorious reveal.

It is only because we live in the death of continuous surrender that we can be forever found in the place of Christ's resurrection.

Jesus Christ is the only thing worth a *life of dying*. Jesus is this "only thing" that is worth being crucified for daily. The most powerful, loving, compassionate, righteous, and innocent man to ever walk the earth was the incarnation of a God who willfully bore our humanity in order to bring us to Him. His desire is to give all of Himself to us, to be loved and experienced so much so that He becomes our very expression.

We need to know we can trust His intentions for our future. Because He is God, and was before the earth was even formed, we can trust *His ability* to deliver compassion. Because He loved us when we weren't deserving, we can trust *His desire* to be compassionate. Because Jesus was the guarantee for both God's ability and desire toward us, it is worth it to still love those who've hurt us in hopes they might discover this same incredible God. Because He forgave us, it is worth it to forgive those who cause us pain and violate us. Because Jesus gave up His place in heaven so that we could join Him there, it is worth it for us to surrender our place in line for the sake of another's promotion.

Jesus walked a life saddled with scorn and hatred in order to bring peace and redemption to His own ungrateful creation. He saw it worthy to unite us to God so He could have us partake in His eternal life and enjoy communion with us forever. Because of Him, because Jesus Christ has found us worthy of His own blood, death, life, and eternity in resurrection, it is worth it to walk through this life offering ourselves in the same way for others. ***God is so rich in mercy, and he loved us so much.***[56]

In Romans chapter 8 and verse 18, Paul said, "For I consider that the sufferings of this present time are not worthy to be compared with the glory which shall be revealed in us." Paul experienced a life by the Spirit in relationship with Jesus even after being responsible for horrifying persecution of Christians. He saw the glory of God revealed in the earth despite being "the chiefest of sinners,"[57] in his own words. Paul said the sufferings of his life couldn't compare to that glory of which he spoke.

> **Jesus walked a life saddled with scorn and hatred in order to bring peace and redemption to His own ungrateful creation.**

There was a time in life where a statement like that made no sense to me. At best, what I imagined when reading verses like this was some sort of cosmic euphoria that I might someday experience if I went far enough or deep enough into Christianity. There were moments and glimpses when words like this would inspire me, either through what I saw as greatness in another person or in something miraculous God did. But personally relating to God revealing His glory through me was always distant and always came with the pressure that I had a lot to learn, a lot to do, and a lot to prove before I could ever arrive.

---

[56] Ephesians 2:4 (NLT)
[57] See 1 Timothy 1:15.

True discipleship was not something I understood very well. I was on the road. I had turned from the world and exposed myself to the Lord. But I still wasn't all that close to Jesus. I often spent more time looking to myself and to others than to Him. Because of that I wasn't so sure of the outcome and His faithfulness to me. I still had my own opinion of what I wanted to look like after the process of following Jesus brought me to the place of "glory." And I still thought I could have a role in determining what the road should look like. I viewed my walk more in terms of a destination than in terms of the actual daily experience of having a living God as my Lord and love, my Father and friend.

> **No one ever told me that the process of discipleship didn't have a destination. Discipleship is the destination.**

No one ever told me that the process of discipleship didn't have a destination. Discipleship *is* the destination. Sadly, I spent years thinking of life as a mission to perfect a religious process and somehow, someday, become a person who liked church, liked Christians, and liked to pray and read my Bible all the time. Or, maybe after enough discipleship I would one day cross over into a higher rank, like *apostleship*.[58] As if the time of learning from Christ would end and I would get to the place where I taught others and met with Jesus every once in a while on a conference call when I needed more power, more authority, or a divine favor.

But who was I fooling? I really only practiced spiritual disciplines when I could muster up the motivation, or

---

[58] I hope you picked up the sarcasm. This thinking is in NO WAY biblical; there is no rank among the children of God, aside from Jesus being the boss....

when the fear of losing my salvation piled up high enough to rise to the top of my priority list...or when I needed something. At that point, in that condition, it would have been a stretch to say I really lived as if Christ was worth dying for. I would have told you He was. And maybe, in fact, I would have actually died for Him. But I was still learning, and often failing, to understand the daily death of carrying my cross. Until the moment when it all changed. ***And you can't take credit for this; it is a gift from God.***[59]

BLOODY BONDS

I am convinced that human beings universally seek only one thing, *aside from power*, that is. No matter how age, culture, status, or religion may separate us, there is a basic desire in the heart of all people to experience authentic relationships. There are many different avenues we walk to bring us to this same point. Family, friendship, careers, religion, and even recreation are almost always individual or corporate attempts to develop relationships. Even in the lives of those who struggle deeply and have been broken by failed human relationships, you often see their success in other areas of life driven by the need to compensate.

On the flipside of overcompensation, some succumb to patterns of victimization that endlessly repeat because they cannot break the cycle of blame and bitterness that cripple them emotionally, mentally, and relationally.

You see, humanity was created to be a part of the Kingdom of God. We have been designed to function as a part of the perfect and holy union that exists between the Father, Son, and Holy Spirit. In the Garden of Eden, Adam and Eve's deepest violation of God was not the breaking of His law, but the violating of their shared fellowship and

---

[59] Ephesians 2:8 (NIV)

communion with the Lord. Eden was created as a space where God and men could exist together in perfect union while at the same time providing His creation the freedom to choose otherwise.

I believe that had Adam and Eve been created as spirit, existing in the realm only God inhabited, they would not have had the space to choose otherwise, and there would have been no freedom to eat of the Tree of Knowledge of Good and Evil. Any rejection of God in that form and realm would have meant instant destruction. Such a violation would have caused a judgment akin to that doled out to Lucifer and his horde.

God gave creation everything it needed to have free and perfect relationship to Him even while being created, and existing "below" Him. The angels were not created to have a destiny of freedom in the same way we are. They attend to the Lord and His family, as even Satan implied in his temptation of Jesus.[60] Remember, when Lucifer rebelled in the place God dwelled, he was permanently cast out. I have to believe the only reason he wasn't destroyed on the spot was that God saw Lucifer and his temptation as a means to sealing our eternal holiness.

In a declaration against Lucifer's rebellion, the human-God relationship actually becomes the standard by which Lucifer is finally judged. Satan's eventual destruction comes by Jesus, the God united to man; the One in whom Lucifer beholds humanity permanently united to the Father in love. We were created lower than angels,[61] yet we've been given the eternal reward Lucifer tried to gain by theft.

---

[60] Refer to Matthew chapter 4:1-11.
[61] Refer to both Psalm 8:4-6 and Hebrews 2:6-8 for more on this.

God's selflessness comes alive in us as we are eternally married to Christ,[62] while Lucifer, in his quest for selfish personal glory, watches it all from the place of eternal death and isolation. Do you see why Satan hates us? A person with the life of Christ, who has the authority to subjugate the spiritual kingdom of death, is Satan's ultimate shame.

Unfortunately, like Lucifer, Adam and Eve chose personal gain over the protection of their relationship with God. As much as they sinned against a holy God, Adam and Eve violated love and chose to embark on a journey of life through self-determined personal growth. Tragically, thousands of years of human history have unfolded in this futile quest as mankind apart from the Spirit has sought to overcome death on our own terms. Ironically, in our quest for independence from God, we find ourselves slaves to the rage that hides in our own hearts, rooted long ago in an act of agreeing with the serpent.[63] *For they exchanged the truth of God for a lie, and worshiped and served the creature rather than the Creator.*[64]

> **A person with the life of Christ, who has the authority to subjugate the spiritual kingdom of death, is Satan's ultimate shame.**

But we know that flesh can only give birth to flesh. It is only the Spirit that can birth supernatural eternal life. And for this reason there is, and has been, but one true

---

[62] Scripture reveals continuously that the relationship God created us for would culminate in that of a husband (Christ) and a bride (the Church); see, among others, Isaiah 54:5; John 3:29; 2 Corinthians 11:2; Ephesians 5:25-27; Revelation 19:7-9; 21:2,9.

[63] Referring to the depiction of Satan from Genesis 3.

[64] Romans 1:25 (NASB)

Kingdom mission. The Lamb was slain before the foundation of the world[65] for one purpose: to restore perfect union to the family of God.

If John the Baptizer's emergence in the wilderness was the preparation for the arrival of Jesus, there was also a great history of God developing His people in order for the Son to be presented in the flesh at the appropriate time. The Scripture mentioned above tells us that Jesus was "the Lamb that was slain before the foundation of the world."[66] If you think about what that means, you are faced with the fact that God must have foreknown the cost of a love relationship with His creation. And although we, as a created people existing in the midst of a fallen world have felt the pain of that heavy cost, there is none who went into that transaction with more to lose than God Himself.

> **There is no union with the Father apart from union with His Son.**

God prepaid for our access and closeness to Himself with something like a "redemption clause" that would result in Jesus's blood being poured out to satisfy any, and every, objection that sin could make to our eternal union. Since Satan had been rejected and cast out of heaven, eternally separated from God, he cannot bear the thought of a "lesser" being experiencing the glorious eternal life of union with God. His plot of deception became a campaign of accusation once humankind sinned. The Spirit-life connection we had with the Father was severed and Satan sought to seize on the rift. ***Your adversary, the devil, prowls around like a roaring lion, seeking someone to devour.***[67]

---

[65] See 1 Peter 1:20.
[66] Revelation 13:8
[67] 1 Peter 5:8 (ESV)

I know the easy out here is to think, *Well, we never asked for this.* No, humanity never "asked in" to this deal. No, we certainly did not have any say in being created; nor did we get a vote in being fashioned with the possibility to fall short of God's intent. This is where many try to opt out of being accountable for judgment. As the object of God's absolute love while having the means by which to share His nature in union with Him, we have been invited into something glorious. This something glorious is a family that far exceeds what primal existence is able to produce. We are adopted into this heavenly family by rightly responding to the Gospel.

Nothing that happens in the Kingdom of God happens apart from God's family. It is the ultimate purpose of Jesus, of the Church, and of the individual walk of discipleship for each of us that the family of God would be redeemed and recreated into the perfect union of the Father, Son, and Holy Spirit. There is no union with the Father apart from union with His Son.[68] There is no union with the Son except by the Spirit. And perfect union to the Spirit means perfect union to all in whom He dwells. Thus, true union to God cannot exist apart from union to each other.

> **True union to God cannot exist apart from union to each other.**

I hope that you are getting this. God has chosen the marriage between His Son Jesus and humanity as the way in which He will completely reveal Himself to creation. He has chosen our marriage to Jesus as the way in which He will judge Satan. But these cosmic happenings are not beyond our daily earthly life. Discipleship weaves us into God's grand plan as we become united to the Spirit while

---

[68] See 1 John 2:23.

living in the earthly realm. This plays out in real-time amongst believers.

In the middle of Satan's tyranny on the earth, where death and darkness seem to have jurisdiction, we partner with God to live in unity and defeat death by declaring the life of Christ is real. We do this by displaying Christ's Spirit alive in us. That declaration is not simple words on the pages of this book. The declaration of the Kingdom in this life is the union of the saints in perfect love—on full display in the power of God and the humility of His nature—through the life of His people. *I am not writing you a new command but one we have had from the beginning...love one another.*[69]

I was hurt by my family. By all of my families. Divorce ravaged us, having begun its work before I was born and hitting home four different times before all was said and done. Who was to blame and how they happened is relevant, of course, to understanding the full picture. Drugs, abuse, and all sorts of unredeemed humanity create the kind of space for broken relationships. In the midst of it, those issues aren't what matters to the toddler, the five-year-old, or the teenage boy fumbling through the fallout of a broken family. By the time I was stepping into my own marriage the shadow of divorce loomed over me as the product of a seed of fear long before buried in my heart. All that mattered then was that the Kingdom—God's power and nature—had not yet brought this area of my life into submission.

My church families were equally dysfunctional. Whether as a kid or a young man, my encounters with churches and the personalities that built (and perverted) them were ultimately the reason I found myself trying to get away from Christianity. I could write a book all by

---
[69] Adapted from 2 John 1:5 (NIV).

itself on the hypocritical church. I could tirelessly expose tendencies and flaws in all forms of ministry because I have personally lived through just about every type of hypocrisy spun and repackaged in the name of God. These distortions are presented as the justifiable byproduct of spiritual gifting because gifts somehow become more important than love for one another. But so many "Christian" things we do are really not Christlike at all, but just "christianesque." We are experts at manufacturing knockoffs to God's artwork.

Oh, and this brings me to another book I could write, the one on the hypocritical self, because it's in me that the true problem is revealed. Whatever hypocrisies we see in this life, and usually the ones we hate most, we are first guilty of. That is why we have no reason to isolate ourselves from the Lord or His church. There is no earthly failure worthy of allowing our lives to be stolen out of God's grace; our pain is not above the price Jesus paid with His blood. No matter who or what we have encountered which has resisted the Kingdom's authority—our family, our church, or our own history—none of it is Jesus's fault, and none of it is reason enough to resist surrendering to His love right now.

It is my prayer, more than anything else in this world, that the experience of this book would take you to a place with Christ that is deeper, stronger, more radical, and more abandoned than you have ever imagined. I want you to walk with Jesus in complete surrender to the One who is true, just, and absolutely in love with you. In my walk with the Lord, this journey has taken me to places I might not have agreed to go had I known the cost or the destination too far in advance. But the Lord is so good toward us, so loving, that even the process He has for us is laid out in a way that pulls us into Him. He has drawn me deeper, and I am just scratching the surface.

I want to encourage you to press on and press in. I want to share some of the places the Lord has taken me and some of the things He has shown me across steps of heartache and success, across experiences of family and career, and across the nations of the earth—all which have drawn me closer to a loving Father than I ever could have wanted. What's more, in His drawing I have been privileged into a life in which my relationships are stronger, deeper, and more authentic than I was ever capable of managing without Him. Discipleship is rending my heart and shaping me to behold the Lord, to carry His love, and to share it with those He has allowed me to cross paths with in this life.

This book is the cry of my heart and, I believe, the cry of God's own heart for you. No matter where you are or where you hope to be one day, I pray you choose the lowest road to the highest place—the one bloody road of true discipleship that leads directly to a life of God's glory shining through you. ***Once you were alienated and hostile in mind, doing evil deeds, yet He has reconciled you in His body by His death, in order to present you holy and blameless before God....***[70]

---

[70] Derived from Colossians 1:21,22.

Part 2

The Gospels

"What only He can do."

3

THE (BLOODY) GOSPEL

THE GOSPEL: AN INVITATION
by Tim Beck
Husband and Father
Founder, Hydrate Student Ministries, Bessemer, AL
Fearless preacher of the Gospel

"Woe unto me, if I preach not the Gospel!"[71]

The Gospel can be summed up in one sentence: Behold the Lamb of God who takes away the sin of the world. The pure, simple Gospel has always been, and always will be, the answer. Jesus told us that if He is lifted up, that all would be drawn to Him. How do we lift up the Lord in our day? Simple. Inhale and exhale the Gospel. Go to the cross and take others with you! There is nothing else to talk about.

Paul, the great apostle, gives himself a very important warning. He was reminding himself and others that the Gospel is what we need to be communicating; and not only communicating, but also continually inhaling and exhaling. Beloved, understand that the Gospel, the Good News—*God's News*—is the very breath of God that should fill our lungs and rush from our lips. In today's culture we

---

[71] See 1 Corinthians 9:16.

are constantly steered towards a path where everything else but the Gospel is being presented and preached. Finding God's News on the nightly news, or in our unrelenting digital news feeds, rarely ever happens. Sadly, many churches fall into this category because the Gospel, at its core, stands against marketable ministries built on life enhancement.

> **The Gospel will never be about man, but will always be about God. And, more importantly, the Gospel is about the God-man, Christ Jesus.**

The Gospel will never be about man, but will always be about God. And, more importantly, the Gospel is about the God-man, Christ Jesus. The truth is we are so consumed with impressing one another, our comfortable lifestyles, and the influence of men, that we've lost the one message that can change us. The Gospel changes everything.

In the name of effective ministry, we consult the latest statistics. We read the latest books on church growth and spiritual equipping. We frantically race to the next conference in search of the next best thing. We structure and restructure small groups in hopes that we have the right "fun" activities this time. Have you noticed that we never seem to stop reaching for magical formulas, manufactured prayers, and the latest preacher on the scene's *keys for revival?* Let me remind us, it's not about the messenger; it's about The Message. The raw, unfiltered Gospel of Jesus Christ is all we need. It's not about what we can do, but about what He did.

Stick with the Book. Tell His story. The Gospel is enough. Jesus's command has not changed. We are to go into all the world and preach…*you've got it*…the Gospel. Revival, church growth, and everything in between will come when we once again start inhaling and exhaling the

Gospel. In chapter 1, verse 16 of his letter to the Romans, Paul reminded the church in Rome that, *"the Gospel is the power of God unto salvation to everyone that believes...."*

The Gospel has power! The Gospel *is* power! What greater power can there be than that which forgives, that which heals, and that which raises a man from the dead? If we want power in our lives, our churches, and our nations, then we must preach Jesus Christ and Him crucified! We must declare that He lived sinless, died, and rose again. We must continue to spread the good news that He was seen alive by over 520 eyewitnesses and is now at the right hand of the Father making intercession for humanity.[72]

Charles Spurgeon once said, "Whatever subject I preach, I do not stop until I reach the Savior, the Lord Jesus, for in Him are all things." Like Paul, Spurgeon is saying we really have nothing to say until we talk about Christ—and then nothing to say after Christ. I pray that we find our message again. I pray that Holy Spirit convicts us like Paul rebuked Peter for compromising the Gospel as he mentioned in Galatians 2; effectively saying, "This is not what saved you! This is not the message delivered unto you! Return to the Gospel!" It is high time we return to, and remain with, the Gospel. I believe the Gospel must take center stage once again and the results will be astounding!

> **What greater power can there be than that which forgives, that which heals, and that which raises a man from the dead?**

Oh, I recall the moment this good news filled my ears and pierced my heart. Radical transformation came on me. Up until that encounter with the Gospel, I lived fifteen

---

[72] See Romans 8:34.

years on the corner of depression and darkness. I was raised in a dysfunctional home and divorce hit when I was eleven. Suicidal thoughts filled my mind as sin took over my life. For the next four years I tried to find hope, joy, and peace in anything the world could serve to me. Nothing worked. Nothing made sense and nothing brought relief. Then the Gospel was preached to me for the first time. That Friday night—in August of 1996—I became a new creation and I found myself permanently captured by and swept into God's beautiful story. The beautiful Gospel.

> **Jesus Christ—that He is, was, and always will be— is the best news ever given to the human race.**

I say it again: Behold the Lamb of God who takes away the sin of the world. Whether for the first time or the millionth time, inhale and exhale the breath of God! As you read the message of the Gospel of Jesus Christ, breathe in deep! Transformation awaits you!

* * *

HIS NAME IS JESUS

There is only one hope. For you. For me. For all of us. There is only one hope and His name is Jesus.

It seems in our church world, understanding the Gospel often begins by undoing many of the extras we have added to the simple message of Jesus Christ. Jesus Christ is the Gospel. "Gospel" is a simple biblical term that means "good news." Jesus Christ—that He is, was, and always will be—is the best news ever given to the human race. He was the best news I ever received—the only news that has brought with it unending hope, healing, strength, and *life to the full.*[73]

Jesus's life, death, and resurrection is the message that God Himself did the hard work in order that I might be found innocent in His presence; that I am deserving of eternal closeness to Him despite my failures, my weakness, and my shame, because Jesus was the sacrifice that paid for all of our sin.

This message has transformed my life and given me what this world is not able to. The Gospel healed me from guilt and pain I felt in regards to the death of my father; it is healing the relationships I spent years tearing apart with dishonesty and unfaithfulness; and has cleansed me of the sin I fell into through drugs, perversion, and other lusts of the heart. The love that Jesus has shown me has been there for me in the absence of healthy earthly relations and taught me to trust that I can lean on Him, depend on His promises, and be a whole person while fully surrendering to His authority over my life.

Over years of His faithfulness I have been, and am still being, transformed into a man who can forgive and love the father I lost—but still honor him in saying that I am not a slave to the curses he never overcame. But it is not this way for everyone. Not everyone accepts the good news, and not everyone is willing to obey a God that doesn't do what they want or expect. Grace both freely gives us access to God and frees us from our own control. To some, there is nothing more dangerous in all the world than the Gospel. ***Anyone who loves their life will lose it.***[74]

---

[73] See John 10:7-10.
[74] John 12:25 (NIV)

By just about every measure, Christianity is under more persecution globally than any other religion.[75] At the time of this writing, conservative estimates say that somewhere between 80,000 and 150,000 Christians will die worldwide this year, simply for their faith. Our faith was birthed under persecution, consecrated by the blood Christ shed on the cross, which Scripture says continues to declare innocence[76] to those who receive Christ as the Lord. Simultaneously, Christ's blood decrees guilt to those who betray His act of love with self-glorification and the idolatry of other gods. Yet the wisdom of God has been rejected from the beginning of our free will kicking in.

John tells us the reason we reject Christ, who is the good news, is because Christ is light and coming to Him means our dark and hidden places must be exposed. How silly. As if God doesn't already know what is to be found under the masks and veils we wear. It's simply pride. It is the pride that we hold on to in not wanting to face or surrender our own darkness that causes us to reject Jesus. Second Corinthians 4, in verses 3 to 5, says that those who do not believe the Gospel have been blinded by "the god of this world" because our faith is in ourselves and the systems we have created which hide us from the light of Christ. For some who say they believe, the same pride refuses to live a "crucified" life before Him that is continually exposed, cleansed, and filled by His presence.

---

[75] A January 2013 article in the leftist *The Huffington Post* titled, "The Most Persecuted Religion in the World," cited a report by Rupert Short, author of *Christianophobia: A Faith Under Attack*, which confirmed more Christians live under persecution than any other people group.

[76] In Genesis 4, Abel was killed by his brother and Scripture refers to Abel's blood crying out for justice; in Hebrews 12, reference is made to the blood of Jesus which speaks a better message: that by faith in Christ we are pardoned from sin.

You see, once we acknowledge Him and we're exposed for who and what we truly are, there can only really be one response. Acknowledging Jesus as the perfect gift of peace from God, which restores us to a right relationship with our Creator, Father, and Lord, means we must align our lives to Him—or in refusing, order our own spiritual death by continuing in rebellion and sin. ***Whoever lives and believes in Me shall never die.***[77]

Just take a look around. Where is the wisdom of men? Thousands of years of history have proven nothing but that we are finding more arrogant ways of claiming progress. Three seconds in front of the mirror is all it takes to find cracks in the foundations of *our* world. The Gospel is the only salvation message because it is the only *living* message that requires a *living* savior. If our lives and history really prove anything, it is that we desperately need a savior.

> **The Gospel is the only salvation message because it is the only living message that requires a living savior.**

If we have no savior, surely we are damned. If no one can redeem us from ourselves, if no one can cleanse us from our sin—if there is none who can rescue us from our own darkness—then there is no reason for living. In the arrival of Jesus, all of creation was extended a promise that the gap between God and man has been bridged. The Gospel is the message that our sin is overcome and our shortcomings cannot separate us from the eternal God. Because Jesus was able to be everything we cannot, and was still willing to bear the punishment we deserve, we have the opportunity to live in eternal union with the infallible God. But only

---

[77] John 11:26

on His terms. In the Gospel we are shown that His terms are perfect love.

Hopefully, by now it is clear to you that this book on discipleship isn't a manual on how to make disciples. It also is not a point-by-point plan on how you can become a great disciple. There aren't even such things. A disciple either is, or is not. Just the same, a Christian should be one who has turned to follow Christ. All others need not even defile His name. You see, in both equations there is one thing that never changes. Christ is never variable. He is eternally the same. And though the flavor of our expressions may differ, what never does is the One whom we follow and the destination He is leading us to.

Even the speed at which we develop, the things we struggle with or walk victorious in, and the gifts we may or may not exercise, aren't the truest measures of a disciple. A disciple is measured by one thing—Jesus. Is Jesus present? Is Jesus *the One* defining and marking our lives in more than words and Sunday activities? Are we instead setting the terms and asking Him to bless us? Hopefully, by now you know that this book on discipleship is more about Jesus and the process of becoming close to Him than some form of guide on how to do it "right." **He who loves Me will be loved by My Father, and I will love him and manifest Myself to him.**[78]

Discipleship is better experienced than explained. That should be no surprise since the same is true of Jesus Himself. But how is it that we experience Jesus? What does it look like for a person to encounter the risen God who is simultaneously here among us, dwelling within us, seated in the heavens next to the Father, and invisible? Well for starters, we must recognize that we need all of that to be true.

We must recognize that we need Him.

---

[78] John 14:21

Once we recognize that we need Him, Christ is faithful to make Himself available to us by the Spirit and through people whose life is found in Him. The Holy Spirit is called revealer, guide, comfort, teacher, counselor, and advocate. All of these titles express the ways in which He interacts with us as we respond to His beckoning.

It is within the Gospel that we find everything we need to gain access to these interactions with the Spirit. Within the Gospel we find everything we need in life. The keys to peace, joy, and happiness are all in one place. In the place where your life—no matter what the circumstances that have led you to this moment—can be declared innocent and worthy to be redeemed by God Almighty, all doubt, fear, and the limitations of this life are thrown off. God is real and He made a way for you to find His eternal purpose while giving you the ability to possess everything you need to accomplish it. What then could possibly stop that from happening? ***Because I live, you will live also.***[79]

DEFINITION

Let's take a moment to get a little technical and be sure we are on the same page, both literally and figuratively. In simple terms, I would explain the Gospel like this: *There is hope for sinful man beyond the sentence of death because of a God who is both good in nature and great in ability. Jesus Christ, in His life, death, and resurrection, is the perfect display and guarantee of this God, and faith in Jesus and His grace gives us access to all that God is—starting right now—if we turn from ourselves and follow Christ.*

I think it is important to have the clearest picture of the Gospel we can. So before we move forward, let's expand on

---

[79] John 14:19

this so we can more clearly see the implications of what a human collision with the Gospel actually looks like.[80]

1. Mankind is flawed and sinful, and by nature unable to do anything about this. If you doubt this, pick a spot in history and you will quickly find a human story of failure, death, and destruction that we retell as one of conquest, progress, and growth. Should you still not believe me, just look in the mirror.

2. God is eternal and perfect—as nothing else is—and His holiness demands that anything less than perfect not be allowed to exist eternally as only He can. Think about it; if things "below" the holiness of God weren't judged and just allowed to exist forever with Him, what would even make Him God? This requires less faith than we think, and simple logic can look at the world around us and realize there must be a genesis to all things and a standard that holds it all together. Without this, there would be no reason to exist, let alone exist righteously. If that's the case this conversation isn't even worth having.

3. Jesus—the perfection of God lived out as a man inhabited by the Holy Spirit—is the expression of God that bridges the eternity-sized gap between God and humanity. Jesus humbly lived as one of us, submitted Himself to our rejection and judgment, bled and died as a once-and-for-all punishment to satisfy all of our sin, and then was raised by God to live again because of His innocence. In doing this, Jesus literally bound us to God and not only spares us judgment, but offers us the empowerment to live as He did in this world. Really think about this one. Not only are we saved, but as Jesus the man was filled by the Holy Spirit of God, He declares that it is possible

---

[80] Suggested reading on the subject of the Gospel: *The Explicit Gospel*, by Matt Chandler and Jared Wilson. I have drawn much in defining the Gospel from this volume.

for all mankind to walk by that same Spirit. This is now the unequivocal standard for human potential.

4. Choose. Either the Gospel is true, and if so, it demands only one response; or the Gospel is a lie and isn't worth paying attention to. If any part of it is false, all of it is worthless. Conversely, if all of it is true, there is not only hope, but also a glorious destination for fallen humanity.

So let's try to boil this back down. 1) CONDITION: The Gospel tells us that people are stained and broken and cannot offer anything more than temporary fixes which will eventually crumble and fade, just as we all will physically perish. 2) NEED: It tells us we need something beyond us—a god or a savior—in order to fix us and answer the cry from within to live beyond the ability of this world. 3) PROVISION: In Jesus's life, death, and resurrection, is seen the only picture of a God both able *and* willing to not only do this, but who *has done this,* to prove it is possible and worth the cost. 4) RESPONSE: Anything other than following such a God-man is a prideful denial that He is good, He is able, and He has done what the Gospel declares.

BORN SKEPTICS

Look, there are things contained in the Gospel that are hard for the human mind to grasp. The terrible realities of evil and the disappointment of failure in this life rage against the notion of such a forbearing and loving God. This world is constructed on principles and systems that try to usurp the authority of God while at the very same time reaching to deny He even exists. Do you see the ignorant hypocrisy in that? If we can disprove God, or at least the parts of His nature that the Gospel demonstrates, we can relieve the need to be accountable to Him and take responsibility for our present condition. But this is why faith is a requirement of coming to God.

Think about it. The author of Hebrews wrote that in order to come to God we must first believe He exists and, even more, believe He is good.[81] In seeing who Jesus was, what He did, and how He calls us into union with Him, both of those previous statements are proven true. If we reject the Gospel it is because we either don't believe it is true, or we reject that it is good. Plain and simple.

How else could selfishness and ambition deal with God than to try to deny Him? Is it any wonder that the general disposition of man before God is one of blaming and rebellion? What we do to ourselves—to our parents, bosses, civil servants, and even governments—we do to God as well. There's no escaping the primal human disposition of people to rage against authority. You don't need an Ivy League research team to prove my point.

Have a baby. Hang around little children. They'll show you how easily what we call "innocence" mixes with selfishness. They'll show you how often the human nature likes to take responsibility for failure. We all want someone to blame. Misery loves company. It takes one to know one. We are all born skeptics.

And yet, we all long for more. ***Unless you change and become like little children, you will never enter the kingdom of heaven.***[82]

COMING IN HIGH

No matter where we think we stand, the Gospel finds us all in exactly the same place. Before eternity, everything is small; everything is dying. The best that any of us has to

---

[81] See Hebrews 11:6.
[82] Matthew 18:3 (NIV)

offer God always falls short of who He is. Where the Gospel meets humankind is face-to-face with the reality that our stairway to heaven ends up woefully short. The best material any of us can build with is ourselves. Regardless of what we accomplish, when we compare this life to eternity, all of us are "as filthy rags"[83] before the holiness of God.

> **It's humorous that we look to our own wisdom to prevent death when we can't even reconcile when life begins.**

The reality is that every human creation either lives or dies intermingled with some form of corruption. Humanity truly is a bloody condition. We enter this life in pain and walk through it in suffering. Even the best and most privileged lives are laced with hurt and loss, and inevitably end in death. The entire process is bloody.

In our infinite wisdom and inescapable arrogance, people constantly push towards trying to prove we can alleviate our human condition. Our world's growing intellectual humanism pretends that failure in our own personal struggles with sin can be overcome by focusing on governmental, social, and religious issues. It's humorous that we look to our own wisdom to prevent death when we can't even reconcile when life begins.

By any measure it's obvious that only the fool is capable of planning life's end. Still we try to plan out our "progress" apart from the will of God. Meanwhile, our achievements, however great or small, all end up in the same place when our heart stops beating. Living a good life is a noble thing, but even Solomon, one of history's most successful and blessed men, wrote the entire book of Ecclesiastes declaring that the wisdom and gain of this life is all futile.

---

[83] See Isaiah 64:6.

Meanwhile we groan, longing to be clothed with our heavenly dwelling....[84]

So it is there we all stand, some in tatters and others dressed to the nines. Some of us will arrive at the gates with our bags packed and our legacies in order. Others face the music with meticulous messes laid out as the only thing to show for a life of trying to get it all right. It is in being able to see this bloody human condition that we can begin to understand that the meeting place of God and man is a cross. What stands as quite possibly the rankest place humanity could create, where our depravity reveals itself in justice becoming the very crime that is the vile torture of a cross, is the bloody ground zero where God extends Himself to us in mercy.

What is humanity's natural response to all of this? How do we respond both to the crisis of our brokenness *and* heaven's invitation to stand in the light and be washed? Religion or denial. Either we begin construction of that stairway to heaven with methods of pretending we can do enough good to stand in light of God's judgment, or we bury our heads in the sand and pretend there is no God at all.

Is there a greater statement of our internal bankruptcy and arrogance? Who can stand before the judgment of God? God, in His remarkable love for us, has offered Jesus as a testament to all humankind. Jesus's life, death, and resurrection declare that His power not only *can save* us—but that it *will save* us—and from that very point of salvation His power ushers us into the glorious eternal life that transcends the death and decay of this world. In knowing Jesus alone, we are invited into eternal life. ***I know my sheep, and am known by My own.***[85]

---

[84] 2 Corinthians 5:2 (NIV)
[85] John 10:14

When the term "the Gospel" is used, there is often a host of things the average Christian thinks. Doctrines come to mind about what we need to do to be saved, how saved is enough saved, and what we do after we are finally saved enough. In many cases, whatever Christian topic is being emphasized in church is believed to be the Gospel. For some people the first four books of the New Testament quickly become the theme of the conversation.

There was a time that the term Gospel was confusing to me. I didn't understand the different ways it was mentioned in the Bible. At times the Gospel is just another biblical term. Other times we read about the Gospel of the Kingdom, the Gospel of Jesus Christ, the Gospel of Grace, and so on. Then of course, there are different pastors and teachers, all rendering words and terms with emphasis on different versions of what you would think should be one clear, central idea.

There is one Gospel. Jesus Christ is the Gospel.

But there is one Gospel. The Gospel of Jesus Christ really is specific and simple; it is the Gospel of the Kingdom, and of Grace. Jesus Himself is the whole idea. Jesus Christ is the Gospel. Jesus is the good news that there is a path for every one of us to get to God and to remain with Him for eternity.

The object of this chapter is to explain and illustrate to you how and why the Gospel must be the foundation of a walk with the Lord, and how and why the Gospel then continues to carry us forward as we become more like Jesus. Remember, discipleship is the process by which we are made to be more like Christ. The Gospel is both the reason and the means by which we would even attempt such a lofty aspiration. Right here and now, if you haven't yet, I invite you to respond afresh to the good news that the Gospel brings. ***You did not choose Me, but I chose you.***[86]

RSVP

There is one story in the New Testament that portrays the simple message of the Gospel better, maybe than any other. Famed evangelist Reinhard Bonnke delivers this message in what may be the most moving account of the Gospel message I and millions of others have ever heard. I will do my best to tell that story as it is intertwined with my very own encounter with the good news of Jesus Christ.

As we read John's account of the Gospel, chapter 8 takes us to the story of Jesus as He teaches a small gathering outside of the temple. He is clearly making waves among the Jewish leaders, a common theme in the Christ's life, stirring people with talk of a new kingdom being established and demonstrations of its power in healing, deliverance, and supernatural miracles.

The heat on this particular day borders on unbearable. You've shifted a few times between sitting on the small stone curb that edges the dusty street, kneeling with one leg in the road, and standing against one of the building walls, all to avoid the sun's direct punishment. The stifled air in this place doesn't help much either. But for several moments on end it seems like you totally forget where you are. All of His disciples are here. This time your hopes are set on having Him bless you; and in Jerusalem no less! At the temple!

It feels like such a long while since that first time you saw Him outside your village. Your spirit has folded itself inside out. The truth is it's only been a few short months. But so much has changed. You had to see Him again.

---

[86] John 15:16

Then, just like that, you are reminded exactly where you are as the Jerusalem sun beating on your neck forces you to shift positions again.

Almost without noticing, an angry crowd has landed right on top of this small gathering. So captivated by His words, by that intense look He has while He speaks—you've never seen a man whose eyes call out so many things to you at once—the noise of a stoning mob somehow snuck up on you. As it all comes together you can see one person in the group knew just what was coming. While you were waiting for the Teacher's next word, you realize that Jesus's pause wasn't to make a point in the message. He had spotted the men, stones in hand, dragging her right to Him. Jesus was, it seemed, bracing Himself in a moment of tempered stillness, for the fury about to meet Him.

Before the small mob even arrives you understand what is happening. It's that moment when something you are focusing on goes from slowly mingling with the background to being instantly thrust into the center of a scene playing out before you. You know, the moment when dawn turns to day, or when you're slowly dazing out of a dream and then abruptly you've awakened and been mentally thrust into the business of the morning. In one such instant, the Teacher was speaking so deeply to you and the small gathering around Him. Then, within the span of a breath, it seems this gathering has been swallowed by something that has sought to utterly monopolize the moment.

"Teacher!" a voice, dignified, authoritative, and condescending, cries out. "We caught this woman in the bed of a married man! In the very act!" he decreed, arms waving over the sobbing woman. There was seething hatred in his eyes—this "elder." In his left hand he held a stone the size of a man's fist; his right bore only the accusation as it pointed and waved. There was a strange tenor about him.

Although he accused the woman, it seemed his furor was not really for her.

"You know what Moses demands! The law is clear and she should be stoned!" This temple scribe's posture and tone was that of an orator making a speech, of a teacher himself, forcefully lecturing a class. With his next breath he posed a question to Jesus.

"But what do You say?" he asked.

As the words proceeded from him the woman moaned in grief. Her shame had led her all the way here, and by now your mind had fully caught up to the drama unfolding before you. You're remembering subconsciously hearing her sobs and screams as the men dragged her all the way through the temple square. Those sobs have now strung themselves together in a pitiful moan that sounds as if it's spilling right out of her belly. As she lies there in the dust, she knows the end of these momentary deliberations will condemn her to death.

In all the movement, you cannot help but notice that in your own heart are strange happenings. You've grown up despising women like this. Your mother raised you on old proverbs that warned against her devices. Your father and uncles mocked her kind and taught you the sanctity of choosing the right stone when it was your turn to help bring forth justice and purity.

But the self-righteousness you are used to stroking in moments like this is somehow turning on you. It's as if Jesus's very presence is causing the fibers of your soul to turn on themselves and question everything you know. A moral shudder is causing your conscience to look over your shoulder at the Teacher, as your mind tries to rally you to join the mob which tradition has called your allies.

Jesus never flinched. You never thought He would, but you also weren't quite prepared to see all of this firsthand, the supposed Messiah facing off with the temple elders. In

Jerusalem no less! But steadily, without words, Jesus turns toward the woman, kneels in the dust before her, and begins to write with His finger in the sandy road. As He finishes and draws up off His knee, what He wrote becomes clear. It's obvious to all who read it. Maybe that's why it's hard to pinpoint exactly why it makes you so uncomfortable. Everyone knows the verdict. For a second the temple elders exchange sideways glances, as if to acknowledge they all see Jesus's written judgment, but still uneasy in not knowing what else He might say.

Still the Teacher spoke not. His eyes met those of the woman for a moment. He doesn't waver before her. He's not capitulating to the elders' fervor, nor does He pander to her fear. But when He looked at her it was as if she stopped breathing for a moment. His eyes, despite her shame, stilled and quieted her. Once again, you are caught up by this Nazarene peasant. He's no longer speaking but every move He makes carries an authority and strength the temple elders lust for. The sneer let out by the one leading them testifies to his jealousy.

> **Never in your wildest moments on earth had you seen anything like this. Jesus is a lunatic.**

"Guilty," he jeered, reading the inscription Jesus had imprinted in the sand before her. But before he could step forward and begin the rally to her execution, Jesus stood up in defiance, glared at the elder—stealing his influence over the crowd—and kneels before him to write again on the dusty road.

Never in your wildest moments on earth had you seen anything like this.

Jesus is a lunatic.

Once more the same word emerges in the sand… *Guilty.*

We were not in Nazareth. This was not Jesus's hometown. This man was standing in the shadows of Herod's temple without kowtowing to any of the holy palace's religious sentinels.

Jesus did kneel before the men of the mob, but rather than kissing their rings, His finger inscribed a single decree in the sand before each of them...*guilty*.

Finally, there was the woman—eyes wide and mouth agape, hastily lying back in the dust. Waiting for a moment to run, she's at the same time captivated by the Teacher she now knows is her only hope. Like the rest of us she is strangely mesmerized at the gall this man shows. Jesus implacably established himself between her and the angry mob leader who was just as hastily awaiting the moment to throw his rock of indignation. Yet the justice he brandished was quickly becoming his own personal rock of offense.

Then Jesus spoke, "Let him who has no sin cast the first stone." His words caused a geyser of disappointment to flush your face with tears. The woman wasn't the only one who gasped as she began breathing again. While His disciples seemed oddly accustomed to this several of you in that crowd were witnessing *this Jesus* for the first time.

Conviction, power, and liberty all converged in a flash that no man had ever before demonstrated to you. Then, rather unceremoniously and one by one, the mob starts to break. Each man, one utterly stunned in silence, and the next gnashing his teeth in arrogant defiance, dropped his ammunition and backed away from the gathering. The group was now only one quivering woman larger than it had been before.

God stands with *her*.

Now that the show was over Jesus turned back to face her. This time He knelt and extended His hand to hers. The righteous Teacher gently reached out for the hand of defilement. As she returned the gesture and reached back, Jesus offered a question that crystallized the gentle authority He had moved with since the very first time you saw Him. "Woman, where are your accusers now?"

"Sir," she quietly responds, "there are none."

"Then rise, for neither do I accuse you," Jesus said as He lifted her to her feet. "You are free to go. I free you to go and never sin again." It was right then that you saw Him as clearly as ever. You saw all of the things you had heard Him say materialize in one moment of climax. You saw both the jealousy and hatred of the religious leaders kindled, and their ambitious control crushed, in one instant of His being. You saw clearly what had been swirling in your chest for the last few months since hearing Him in Judea.

God stands with *Jesus*.

And now, *Jesus* is calling out to you....

I cannot say where you find yourself in the story. I remember the shame I felt when I found myself in front of the Lord, sin before me, a young life in shambles. Like the woman in the story, I didn't need anyone to tell me I was guilty. The stones I feared weren't being held by temple leaders. But nonetheless, I remember a place in life where the brokenness, failure, and dirtiness of sin called out to me that I deserved no reprieve from judgment.

From the inside out, voices raged against me. Some were the voices of my parents, some of pastors and preachers, some school teachers, and still some were just echoes that had risen up in my own mind reminding me of the contradictions that I had built my life on. And even when I could temporarily escape the burden of what was wrong in my life, there were no other voices I was able to hear offering me comfort.

I was listening to voices of people I had called my friends, those of people I desperately wished would be friends, and worst of all—my very own voice which mocked me for being fat, ugly, or for not being good enough, smart enough, or cool enough to be wanted. All of the images I portrayed were broken, and from the inside I knew it wouldn't be long before I totally fell apart.

Everything I was had converged to form this manic paradox. I lived a life in two homes. One was the simple, if not at least faithful, Christian home of my single mother. In it, I had incredible experiences through faith and undeniable encounters with God. My mother was humbled in life and always in need of the hand of God. My father was exactly the opposite. He was the most dynamic and independent man I knew. His home was more complicated and faster; the sometimes extravagant home of an ambitiously wealthy, albeit unquestionably loving father.

I learned how to live in both places, and constructed two conflicting realities to live in. I was an honor student, a leader in several capacities; even religiously smooth and confident. At the same time, I was hollow. I chased the satisfaction of my father's approval and success, but somehow lived with the tension that I knew all I could construct with the materials he could give me would expire early. This internal storm led me down a dark path where I turned to anything to numb me. Hope and joy were no longer things I believed I could have. Eventually, I even lost my father, the icon of what I hoped to become, to the same vices I determined to serve.

I needed a savior. Life was serving me a long list of indictments. Religion offered me nothing more than hypocrisy. Like the woman, Jesus offered me His hand, and when I took it, He pulled me up. From the inside out, Jesus purged me of guilt, shame, and cleared me of every lie seeking to stone me in the courtroom of my conscience. He miraculously healed my addiction and quieted my need to be loved, with the permanent fix of eternal life and the acceptance and approval of God Almighty.

Jesus, knowing my guilt, told me that the voices had no power because He stood now as my merciful judge. Jesus paid for me with His own blood that says that I can live innocently on His account. That was the moment of my glorious salvation—first pursued as I cried out for Him under a streetlight in the darkness of my childhood neighborhood—and finally realized just a few months later in a church when the warm presence of God tangibly surrounded and permeated my being like a heavy mist.

> **Jesus paid for me with His own blood that says that I can live innocently on His account.**

But a blatantly lost sinner isn't the only character represented in that story of the woman caught in adultery. There are also the scribes and temple leaders, who unwittingly presented themselves to the Lord of the Gospel in a whole other light. Funny thing is, I have found myself there too. It wasn't long after being saved by the wonderful grace of Jesus that I found myself formally educated in the ways of religion. In my salvation I somehow forgot that it was Christ alone that redeemed me and made me worthy of being called a child of God. I had become professionally religious.

Somehow, I learned to rely on myself. I learned to rely on teaching and instruction. I learned how to rely on sermons and doctrines, on churches and ministries. It was as if, after meeting the goodness of God in a moment which freed me from sin, I had forgotten that it was only His words and power that could carry me forward in my walk. His words to the woman were, "Now go, and sin no more." Because God said so—because God was satisfied that punishing Jesus was enough—Jesus's Gospel continuously declares that we can walk forward from salvation, through this life in glorious victory.

We both know that we rely too heavily on things which surround us. We have so many religious resources and tools. We have plenty other religious leaders and institutions that are perfectly okay teaching us to follow them and their methods rather than staying firmly planted on the message of the Gospel. But we must stay desperately connected to the One who is the living Gospel.

It is so much easier and more comfortable; it is so much less bloody to walk a life of manageable Christian development than to stay constantly in need of Jesus. It requires surrender to follow Him wherever He goes, doing whatever He does. That's why I found myself in need of His salvation all over again, just a few short years later.

> **It is so much easier and more comfortable to walk a life of manageable Christian development than to stay constantly in need of Jesus.**

I wanted recognition as we all do. Like the temple leaders, every one of our human hearts longs to be in the place where we are the one "holy" enough to declare judgment on another. Not because our intention is to cater to evil desires, but because we are brought into a decaying world in which we are taught there's not enough to go around. We learn to take care of number one.

We all want to be righteous, but our human weakness aims for a righteousness that compares favorably to other created beings rather than the righteousness that is perfect in Christ. The Gospel calls us so much higher. Out of the darkness it calls us, into union with Him it calls us, and through all of the life ahead, it carries us. He carries us.

That is, if we let Him. ***You shall be perfect, just as your Father in heaven is perfect.***[87]

COMING IN LOW

Jesus declared that He is "the way, the truth, and the life," and that, "no man comes to the Father except through Me." What exactly was it that Jesus meant with these words? It is pretty simple, actually.

Jesus is the way to the Father. By following Him, learning to be like Him, and living as He lived, we find ourselves both with Him and the Father, through His Holy Spirit living in us.

Jesus is the truth means that His very life answers the penultimate question of life and existence. It means that His words—of which He lived out every last one in selfless compassion, supernatural purity, and miraculous power—are the only words that can define the terms of the universe, and even the only words which can define us.

Jesus is the life means that by engaging in a relationship with Him, we are changed and empowered into being a people who can live above the influence and demand of ourselves and the world we live in. As Jesus is the life, and we live in Him, we live beyond the temporal life this world has to offer and we gain the eternal life of connection to God after this physical life ends.

So which way do we go? Follow Jesus. Where will we find the answers? Listen to Jesus's words. How do we actually live beyond ourselves, and after our bodies pass away? By knowing Him and drawing from supernatural power that dwells in us. ***I am the way and the truth and the life.***[88]

---

[87] Matthew 5:48
[88] John 14:6 (NIV)

Coming to God only happens through Jesus, and this means knowing who and what we are before the Lord. Every one of us is low before Jesus. Nothing can stand before the magnitude of God and the goodness of what He has done for us in Christ. No way of our own which we exchange for His life—no opinion which we regard as truth, and no success—is above what is His.

Just as Isaiah the prophet discovered in meeting the glorified Christ, we are all found to be unclean and everything in us is revealed as beneath Him. Although we may not see Jesus in a vision like Isaiah did,[89] the glorious moment of salvation is just as Isaiah described. In that moment of grace, we discover a lowliness of heart which makes it easier to turn from the sin that tries to keep us pinned down in the mud and turn to the One who lifts us into heavenly places. Staying connected to the Gospel after that encounter is what keeps us in the right place. Isaiah cried out the Lord's words in chapter 55:9 (NIV), "As the heavens are above the earth, so are my ways higher than your ways and my thoughts higher than your thoughts."

Nothing can stand before the magnitude of God and the goodness of what He has done for us in Christ.

We must come before the Lord low, or as Jesus said, "poor in spirit,"[90] and we must continue to walk the same way if we are to truly see the Kingdom of God revealed in our lives. There will be times ahead where we experience great successes or when we are along for the ride while God is on display. In those moments people will always try to give us credit. Both believers and unbelievers alike

---

[89] See Isaiah chapter 6.
[90] See Matthew 5:3.

are much more comfortable praising your achievements than those of the Lord because anything God does keeps everyone humbly in the right place.

Right relationship with Jesus, the Living Gospel, and His Church, keeps us reminded of His beauty, His might, and who we are in perspective to Him. As the "old man"[91] we are unworthy and bound to sin; as the "new creation," who has crucified the flesh and is raised up with Christ, we are worthy because the Gospel made it so. Jesus's death ensured the bill was paid for us to own a piece of God's endless Spirit. Jesus's resurrection ensures that Spirit is delivered without delay.

> **Religion is a charade of comparisons, vanities, and man-made badges of honor with the word "god" painted on them.**

Even as we grow, when we are in continuing communion with Christ, we can see things through His perspective and we grow in grace. Growing in arrogance, comfort, or laziness happens as we take credit for things in life; as we step off of the Gospel and forget our source. Often we begin to try and accomplish things spiritually by simply applying principles and acquiring knowledge. Acting like this only puffs up our ego and distances us from the Lord.

Beware the workings of religious piety which counterfeit the authentic rhythms of a love affair between Jesus and His bride. Religion is a charade of comparisons, vanities, and man-made badges of honor with the word "god" painted on them. Religious activity does nothing but deceive us into believing we can stand before God, head

---

[91] The "old man" refers to the person we are before we enter relationship with Jesus; our crucified self, continuously "put off" as we walk in surrender to Jesus. See Ephesians 4:22-24 and 2 Corinthians 5:17.

held high, because our résumé is going to read better than the next guy in line.

Jesus is the beginning and the end of all things. Scripture tells us He is, was, and always will be.[92] He was before creation, has walked through creation, and will carry creation to an eternal victory. But more than that, more dear to the heart of the God who was a Father before a Creator, Jesus is the God-man who has eternally linked the Father to His children.

In Him who is the way, the truth, and the life, we find the example, the reason, and the motivation for how to be part of a family that this world cannot offer. Everything eternally good that happens is the result of the good news of Jesus Christ. And everything good is possible when we stay connected to Jesus as our "power source" for eternal life—*when we stay low.*

Coming in low means presenting yourself to Jesus, to His simple and perfect good news just as the woman caught in the act of adultery. We come to Him helpless, desperate, and with no strength or support beyond that which is offered us by the hand of heaven. Coming in low means staying in that place, even as we are healed, set free, and built by the power of God into people who can love and live in freedom even with prosperity; as people who never forget what it is like to need His help.

We keep our hearts broken and pure because we know the God that is waiting for those moments to heal us. Rather than trying to lead hurting people to Him by accusation and condemnation, we can beckon the world to our loving Father by ministering the Gospel to them, with our lives being redeemed as examples. **You are the light of the world.**[93]

---

[92] Revelation 1:8
[93] Matthew 5:14 (NIV)

> As long as you set yourself up as a little god to which you must be loyal there will be those who will delight to offer affront to your idol.
>
> —A.W. Tozer, *The Pursuit of God*

4

SONSHIP AND CIRCUMCISION

SONSHIP: AN INVITATION
by Frank Summers
Husband and Father
Counselor, Mentor, and Pastor to many
One who embodies the living relationship of the Son
and the Father

When the Lord created man, we were "formed in the image of God, according to His likeness."[94] We were created to be image bearers...sons...reflections of the nature and likeness of the Father on earth, as it is in heaven. Humanity stood in His presence, exposed to His counsel as He relationally expressed His glory to us. In return, we expressed the Father's design and desire for all creation. At the fall of mankind all of humanity was separated from God by sin, naked and without the reflection of His glory, and this relational connection was lost. Instead of being in His likeness, we became a marred and deformed creation.

At the incarnation of Jesus, the Son came once again to restore fallen mankind to an exact representation of the Father's image. Jesus said if we have seen Him, we have seen the Father. He also came to purchase redemption for His fallen creation, thus restoring us *to* the Father.

---

[94] Refer to Genesis 1 account of creation.

"Sonship" is a word that describes a relationship to a parent; in this case that relationship between Father God and the spiritually recreated "son." The term is important to us because He has made all of us, both men and women... sons in the image of Christ. The Bible clearly states: "... but to all who did receive him, who believe in his name, he gave the right to become children (sons) of God, who were not born of the will of flesh, nor of the will of man, but of God."[95]

> **I had to find healing in the power of God the Father's love for me.**

For many, emotional wounds have been created in early years by fathers who didn't know how to love, or simply weren't present; this creates a lack of understanding of what a father is supposed to be, or how we respond appropriately in our natural and spiritual relationships to our father. This was true for me, personally. I had to find healing in the power of God the Father's love for me.

As this healing was taking place I went through the various stages of spiritual childhood, adolescence, and finally—the mature son—who seeks to reflect the nature and will of his father. In walking with Christ, I grew to understand that Father God intended this relationship to be passed on from one to another. We are to be fathers to others in the faith, reflecting the nature, character, and glory of God. Jesus is the one who modeled this restored relationship for us.

Paul the famous apostle said it this way, "Because you are His sons, God sent the Spirit of His Son into our hearts, and the Spirit cries out, 'Abba Father.' So you are no longer a slave but a child of God, and a joint heir with

---

[95] John 1:12,13 (NIV)

[Christ]."[96] I am humbled and honored at the idea of being an image bearer of God the Father; that He has privileged me with the opportunity, in my limited capacity, to set an example for others to follow. I am reminded of a quote by Paul Silway, "We must remember that we are sons (and daughters) of God, not because we are good but because God is good."[97]

* * *

(RE)BORN BY BLOOD

Sonship is the immediate result of a right response to the Gospel. In whatever terms you would like to use—being born again, regenerated, saved, or made alive in the Spirit—among others, what we are describing is the instantly supernatural experience that occurs when we turn from our allegiance to the world and give ourselves over to Christ.

John's gospel records that night in the garden when Nicodemus secretly came to ask Jesus how it was that He performed miracles and did things only God could do. Jesus answered this way, "…unless one is born of water and the Spirit, he cannot enter the Kingdom of God. That which is born of flesh is flesh, and that which is born of the Spirit is spirit.… You must be born again."[98] The importance of this transfer of identity and all that comes with being transformed from a slave of sin into a child of God is greater than I can possibly encapsulate in one book, let alone this one chapter.

The thread of sonship is eternally long; spun before time, woven throughout human history with God, and

---

[96] Galatians 4:6,7 (NIV)
[97] "Paul Silway, Paul's Quotes," *goodreads,* https://www.goodreads.com/quotes/list/47213612-paul-silway.
[98] John 3:5-7

finally revealed in its entirety in the glorious union between Christ and us, His Church. Jesus declared to Nicodemus that being a child of God was what made Him capable of doing things only God was able to do. With that in mind, in the coming pages I will highlight some of this divine drama in order to give a current context to our experience of sonship—the ultimate place I hope this chapter leads you in relationship with the Father.

STILLBORN

Into this world we are born with nothing more than the ability to survive. At best, that can barely even be considered an ability. We require constant care; and an infant's survival in this life relies on others whose abilities are limited at best. Survival often means learning to make hard choices, choosing ourselves over others and putting limits on what we will sacrifice for others. Despite momentary glimpses of valor that we write into our history books and teach kids to aspire toward, the permanent condition of a heart not subjected to the influence of the Gospel is one after personal gain or, at the very least, survival at all costs.

Death in this life really results in eternal life for anyone connected to God.

That is because our spirits are born disconnected from the reality that beyond our physical death we are called to live forever. We are born primal creatures, detached from the reality that death in this life *really results in eternal life* for anyone connected to God. In essence, we arrive in this world spiritually stillborn. ***Unless one is born of water and the Spirit.***[99]

---

[99] John 3:5

I often preach that no matter where we stand with the Lord, no matter what we seek or what we feel called to, and no matter how strong or weak we feel before Him, if we cannot wholeheartedly say we have encountered the love of God as that of a perfect Father, then there is no more important place to go. I tell people, "Do not pass 'Go' and do not collect $200," in reference to the famous board game Monopoly.

It is right here, at the point that we meet Him as *Daddy God*, where we unlock the most rewarding experience in knowing Him. It is when we learn to knock on the door to the Father's heart where we are shown the safety and relational intimacy that binds us to Him, guards us against our own hearts, and prepares us to be formed in a way that we can truly be poured out *for* God's family and *with* God's own heart. We can only continue to walk in victory over death as we continually experience life. And we only continually experience life when we learn to live as needy children dependent on an immeasurably loving Father.

GROWING YOUNG

I have alluded already to some of the ways that my relationship to my earthly father has influenced me and shaped much of my life. There is really no way I can tell my story without at some point talking about him. John Bruce Garrett was the greatest man I ever knew. Although he was successful, I've known many who achieved more. Although he was smart, I've known many who were smarter. Although my father was handsome, I've known many just as good-looking.

Despite all of the things he accomplished, all of the gifts he was bestowed, and all of the ways he loved on me, my father had just as many failures; falls even greater than his victories. But he was my dad. And for a period in my life there was no one I wanted to be with more, no one I wanted to be like more, and no one I thought more capable of anything in the world than him.

Being his son made me feel invincible. But it was only in my childhood innocence that I viewed life that way. Now, all these years later, I have had time, experience, and age to counsel my opinions. I cannot honestly say that I believe he was the greatest man to ever live by any universally measurable metric. But I still love him and long for him beyond any other. Because of redemption and healing I can look back at the ways his failure hurt me while still being able to love him, and still to this day I remember and desire his love for me.

> **Our view of God is being marred by the imperfections of this world.**

But now there is a certain longing to be like him and to emulate him—a safety and security in who he was to me then—that no longer exists. I now know who he was in a light I never understood as a child. Honestly, aside from the redemption that the Lord has brought into my life and the healing that has taken place in my mind and heart, that "mature" knowledge isn't totally a good thing. The knowledge I have of both the good and evil sometimes threatens to stain the joy I hold onto when I view the past. It's that past and my experience with a fractured fatherhood that worked its way into a place of my heart which tainted my understanding of the Lord.

It is very important that we recognize when our view of God is being marred by the imperfections of this world. We need to be able to see the ceiling we set for His goodness and nature because we have allowed pain, fear, and skepticism to write the boundaries for us.

For many, history with their father doesn't come with the same stains. Not everyone, hopefully not even the majority, would say their history with their dad is laced with hurt and pain. Many can joyfully say that their father has walked them through life in a relationship of love that embodies peace and wholeness, and still more continue with their father in healthy relationship today. But even if that is the case, all of our life on this earth is not so. Sooner or later, the business of life, the hardship of survival in this world, and the callousness of life's pace creeps into the fabric of who we are.

Ultimately, the emotional and relational dynamics of "growing up" overtake all of our relationships, especially the one we were created to have with our spiritual Father in heaven, where faith and a certain bewilderment are prerequisites.

As we grow up, we acquire the skills of independence. We learn to go it alone and to share intimacy in less open, more guarded ways. In most cases, we "grow out" of the need to experience the daily love and affection of a father. We grow calloused to relationships in which we are free to be totally needy and at the same time unabashedly loved by someone we completely adore, fear, and obey.

Our human tendencies don't lean toward investing whatever spiritual capital we keep through the process of losing our innocence in a person we can't see and touch. For this very reason, the work of the Gospel, which declares to us that Jesus granted us a pardon from the sin that keeps us out of the presence of God, also awards us the honor of being called God's children. As His children, we are therefore entitled to be with Him, to be like Him, and to inherit everything a perfect heavenly Father could possibly bestow upon His kids.

The Holy Spirit is on a mission to make sonship, first a right to identity because of what Jesus did, into an experience that cements in our hearts God's place as our Father and us as His beloved children. ***He will take of what is Mine and declare it to you.***[100]

No matter what our earthly perspective is on fatherhood, life in this world separates all of us from a certain part of God and His character which must be restored in order to know God and experience Him in the way He has intended. "Man cannot live on bread alone, but on every word that comes forth from the mouth of God."[101] Or how about, *man cannot live on nourishment alone, but on hearing, experiencing, and knowing the nourisher.* Or we could say, *man cannot live on principles alone, but on a deeply intimate connection with the Lord where we know and hear His voice.* Or better yet, *it's not good enough to know the Bible and have a good life, but we only truly have eternal life when we are in a living relationship with the Lord in which we hear His words as He speaks them to us.*

When Jesus said that in order to inherit the Kingdom of God we would need to become like little children,[102] this is what He meant. Being like "grown-ups" before God, where we call on Him when we need Him, and where we live in a relationship built on the value what we can do for each other, is not worthy of the Father's great love for us. To literally lay hold of His Kingdom, of all that He is, all that He has, and all that He influences, we must be needy and intimate, bold and unafraid, vulnerable and with nothing more than the ridiculously innocent awe a child holds for their invincible father.

---

[100] John 16:14
[101] Matthew 4:4 (NIV)
[102] See Matthew 18 for more on this subject.

DADDY

Along the way in my walk with Jesus, there have been moments where I have been either shown or told things which have altered the course of my life. As I remember those occasions, there are two things that stand out to me as part of each of those life-changing moments: In every case what the Lord communicated dealt with who I am in His sight; and every time it instantly drew me closer to Him than I had ever been before.

> **The best view I had of Father God was cosmic, distant, and unapproachable.**

The walk of a disciple of Jesus must involve these incredible moments of discovery where our own insufficiencies are met with the overwhelming love of a Father who sees past those shortcomings, reveals the value He has placed on us, and then draws us directly to His greatness. Experiencing an eternally great Father who perfectly loves us is the fountainhead of strength and confidence which propels us to live above the fear of punishment and death in this life. Let me share some of how this dynamic in relationship is unfolding for me.

For years of my life, the best view I had of Father God was cosmic, distant, and unapproachable—as a kingly father ruling His "children" much the way He managed planetary orbits and judged the angelic realm. Needless to say, although I knew the Scripture and the language of the "Father in heaven," relating to Him was a whole different ballgame.

I always felt I could get to Jesus; like on some level the Son might actually want to walk around with me, imparting Himself to me as He did the the Twelve Disciples. Even with Holy Spirit, as weird as I sometimes thought He was in my ignorance, and as confused as I often felt about exactly who He was and what He did, Holy Spirit still felt like a part of the Trinity who really wanted to show up and have some fun once in a while.

God the Father was always a different story. Reconciling the awesomely powerful Creator, the immovably holy Judge, and *my* Father in heaven, who actually heard my voice as it cried out, rather than reading my prayers when they made it high enough up the divine priority list, was an altogether impossible task. He was too big for me because I still wasn't worth seeing. He was too busy for me because I wasn't doing anything important enough. Most of all, I couldn't view myself as the son that God, the authority who governs the universe, was interested in. In my view, I was trapped because there were far too many "issues" I needed His help with fixing before He would even *want* to help me.

Then, almost instantly, everything changed. At the time, I was spending an hour every Friday morning with my pastor. That, in itself, was a miracle. This pastor was becoming close to me as a mentor despite an encounter years earlier which had led to an offense in my heart. At our first encounter, he referred to me as "son," a grave violation of my emotions and ego. He then asked me a question about my walk with the Lord, which of course I took personally. However, years later, having been humbled by a very painful event in my family, I was led with my wife to seek counsel. This pastor and his wife had been through the same crisis and we reached out for help.

When we met, they poured love and compassion on us and helped my wife and me manage our grief. Before we left his office that day, I felt the Lord speak to my heart that I was to apologize and confess my offense. When I did, he instantly dismissed it as water under the bridge and no offense on his part, and then invited me to spend time together whenever the opportunity arose.

Within a short period of time God's direction moved us back to the local area of his church and we started regularly attending there. While he was becoming our pastor, we began to meet weekly over breakfast at Wendy's. Consider this one of the Lord's first gentle nudges toward healing a place in my heart that for years had rendered me unable to get close to my heavenly Father.

On one particular Friday morning, I can remember asking a question related to my "growing" in ministry anointing in order that the Lord could use me more. At the time I was in Bible college and was trying to align my life with the call my wife and I felt for missionary work in Africa. I was looking for pragmatic pointers on how to be better prepared for the ministry. Pastor answered me, and then I recall him asking if he could share something he felt was prophetically from the Lord in regards to my life. Of course, I inclined.

"John," he said, "I feel led to tell you that the Lord is going to show you exactly what it means to be His son. You have desired more than anything else to hear Him say, 'Well done, my good and faithful servant,' but what I hear from Him is, 'This is my beloved son, in whom I am well pleased.' He then looked at me and said, "This isn't one you will figure out on your own, but the Spirit of God is going to sovereignly reveal this to you in a way that heals you and transforms your heart."

We left that morning as we did any other. I was always blessed and gracious for him giving me his time, and I listened to everything he said. I remember that there wasn't any great sense that day that I had heard some earth-shattering prophecy. But I did leave asking the Lord that if this was from Him, to do exactly as Pastor had said. My spirit stirred because I couldn't deny that inside my heart were open wounds which I had long covered with hard work, independence, and misguided passion. Thankfully, this was one prayer it wouldn't take the Lord long to answer.

The very next day, a summer Saturday morning in 2010, I left the house for work. Back then I was cooking and helping manage a pizzeria about forty-five minutes away from home. It had been about twelve months since I let go of the last of the "things," including my mortgage broker job, which I gained and lost as part of the 2008 banking bubble crisis.

I began to pray one of those "God, maybe" prayers—you know the kind you pray when you don't feel like you deserve being heard. They are the kind of prayers you pray when you don't want to offend God because you know the only times you're talking to Him are when you're groveling for something. So as I began to spiritually whine to God, trying to qualify each request, I heard a quiet, yet steady voice speak to my heart....

> **You don't want to offend God because you know the only times you're talking to Him are when you're groveling for something.**

"Tell your Daddy you love Him."

Honestly, I didn't really know how to respond. The voice spoke from within. What the voice said, coupled with the sure and unshakable tone that didn't exist in any of the usual voices that had my attention, made it clear this was not my own. I sort of scowled and stuttered back an internal reply.

I'm not saying that, I thought.

Then again He repeated, a little stronger, yet with the same delicate sturdiness and care as He spoke with a second earlier, "Tell your Daddy you love Him."

Explaining what was happening in me is almost impossible. But my response to Him in that moment revealed the condition of my heart. "I don't have a daddy," I quietly mouthed back to the Voice. "My daddy died a long time ago," I said. "And I am a grown man. I don't even use the word daddy. My girls call *me* Daddy." I was verbalizing my pain as a protest to what I was being asked to do.

And then I remember the tears began to pool in my eyes as my emotions culminated in one last refusal of the Lord. "You can't possibly want *me* to call *You* Daddy."

Daddy was a loaded word for me. It was way too close. I had a hard enough time with "Father." I certainly wasn't looking for a dad. It had actually become a very convenient barrier between me and the Lord to have this void in my heart which couldn't be filled by anyone else. For years the place my father vacated was protected because I knew no one could replace him. I projected that same defense on people like my pastor as a way to write off the things I didn't want to hear from them. Using the word "Daddy" directly toward the Lord would give Him an exclusive place within the innermost chambers of my heart. It would ruin my ego and undo my long-developed identity.

The tough, self-determining man I was building would never call someone "Daddy." Apart from the deepest intimacy and affection, which I clearly didn't have with God, "Daddy" actually sounded silly in my own mind; it could only be contrived. In fact, the only time daddy was a useful word was when my little girls wrapped all of their love in it and poured it out on me. And really, it only worked for them because they were mine. Hearing someone else's kids call me "Daddy" would be just as strange as me calling my father's replacement by it.

And right there is where the swirl of emotions and my racing thoughts ground to a screeching halt. The reality of the Father's invitation to address Him with this one word—*Daddy*—meant something that touched the deepest recesses of my heart. I cried as I said to Him, "You can't possibly want me to call you Daddy!"

Without hesitation I felt Him say, "Yes, I do."

In that moment my heart realized what it meant for the Lord to ask me this. He wasn't asking me to bow. God wasn't asking me to salute. He didn't ask me for a résumé, a completed checklist, or even to acknowledge Him as God. The God of eternity, *the One who formed the universe* had just told me that His love for me was akin to what I felt when I opened the front door after being gone all day at work. My Father God had asked me to give to Him what my little girls give to me as they bolt to the door, arms wide open, screaming, "DADDY!" The way I look at them and long for that abandoned and unashamed love was the way God's heart was positioned toward me.

> **Everything the Lord is and everything He has is the inheritance of His children.**

Let me say, in the deepest, sincerest way that I can convey in words, that this understanding of the Lord and how He sees you—beyond any other revelation—changes everything in the life of a disciple of Christ. Paul described Jesus as the "firstborn" of many children. Malachi prophesied that with the Messiah would come the restoration of the relationship between the Father and His children;[103] Isaiah declared that through the coming of a Son would come the Kingdom of God;[104] and in that *relationship of sonship with God*, He would restore the order of heaven to creation. The Psalms[105] cry out that through the Son the

---

[103] See Malachi 4.
[104] See Isaiah 9.
[105] See Psalm 2.

nations are promised justice, and that with honoring the Son comes the forbearance and blessing of the Father.

Now again, I understand not everyone comes to the Lord with the same issues I had. But this world and the enemy are set on destroying the intimacy between the Lord and His children in any way possible. Every bit of skepticism we accrue on the journey of life is an affront to absolute transparency and perfect intimacy with our eternal Father.

Wherever you have gained disappointment, the enemy has sought to compound it into an internal flinch that adds just one tiny step you'll take in your heart before speaking with your Father. He is bent on distorting your ability to hear from Him, and to hinder you from just entering a place of intimate stillness before Him without having to question whether or not He wants to meet you there. Everything the Lord is and everything He has is the inheritance of His children. A few of these little steps added to our lives over time create a distance, however small, from the promises and experiences the Lord desires for you. ***Satan has desired…to sift you as wheat.***[106]

BE LIKE THEM

The entire exchange that unfolded in the story I just shared with you occurred in about the first seven or eight minutes of that Saturday morning commute to work. For the next half hour or so my heart opened wide to a dialogue with a God who was revealing to me, on the spot, a glimpse of the vastness of His love and desire for me as His child.

I laughed in a way that was unbridled like I couldn't remember. I was liberated to cry tears of freedom that felt as if they cleansed me while they fell. I asked questions

---

[106] Luke 22:31 (KJV)

that weren't laced with doubt about whether or not they'd be answered or with a hidden demand for the answer I wanted. The whole experience was as if I was being filled in a way that forced a certain purging at the very same time. I was like a Styrofoam cup having its bottom blown out by a fire hose.

At some point the Lord brought me into what I would call a vivid daydream. Never mind that I was driving. What occurred was a mixture of that gentle voice sounding across my chest and a mental illustration that played out in my mind's eye. I heard the Lord say to me, "Let Me show you My son, John." As He spoke I saw myself as a young boy.

> **I was like a Styrofoam cup having its bottom blown out by a fire hose.**

"Every morning you get out of bed and do your best to get everything right. From the minute you wake up, you are diligent to make your bed, be sure your room is neat, and dress appropriately for the day ahead of you." Clearly, the Lord was speaking figuratively. I hadn't physically made a bed more than ten times in six years of marriage.

He continued, "Like a good kid, you eat breakfast, clear your plate, and move on to the next task. I watch you work hard to try to get it all right." It's funny, even now as I share this, I can remember a lot of what it felt like to see it unfold the first time. I remember noticing the intensity in my face and the tension in my demeanor as the young kid I was seeing in this daydream tried so very hard. It was like I was able to see, in this picture of myself as a child, the very pressures and feelings that I had been carrying throughout my day-to-day life.

"At the end of the day, after everything's done and you're ready for bed," the Voice continued, "that boy doesn't always come to say goodnight to Me while I'm sitting there on the couch. With that son," He said, "John, the way you come to Me all depends on how you believe you've done that day." Again, I saw the conflict in myself playing out on the boy version of me in the scene Daddy was describing.

"When you've gotten everything right, when it's all gone well, you come to Me and ask for your allowance. You tell me all the things you've done to earn My approval and why you think I will want to make good on My promises to you. And in response, I hand those rewards you seek over to you from time to time, according to your expectation.... But," the Voice went on, "when it doesn't go well, you hesitate to ask. Sometimes you don't even come. You see, that son has formed a certain relationship with Me and I have met him in that place; but it is lacking. Aside from what you think you can do or deserve, you don't really believe that I want you."

He was right; dead on, in fact. That's normally the way it is when the Lord speaks to my heart.

"Now let me show you another son, one who looks a lot like your little girls." Immediately what I saw was the same picture replaying itself. "This son," the Father continued, "gets out of bed wanting just as badly as the first to do everything right. But he doesn't. First thing in the morning, he steps out of bed and onto the toy he left out the night before. And when he trips and burns his knee on the carpet, he immediately calls on Me to hold him. And I do, even when I need to correct him."

Like in the first picture of myself, I could see the emotions this boy version of me carried. But they weren't heavy. They were soft, even a bit naïve. Then Lord continued to narrate this picture in my mind. "You see, this son, as hard as he tries, seems to miss so much. But like your girls, he relies on Me to remind him to clear his breakfast plate, to rinse the dishes before they go in the dishwasher, and to make his bed before he goes out of the house." The tone that the Voice spoke with continued in a steady, reassuring way. It kept me perfectly safe as it exposed things in my heart I had never quite looked directly at before, even if I knew somewhere inside that this was the reality of my heart before the Lord.

"But the thing is, this son isn't afraid to be My son, and like your girls, his heart toward Me is focused on other things." This picture was creating in me a deep appreciation and longing at the same time. "John," the Voice went on, "at the end of the day, when it's time for bed, the difference between this son and the son you have become is that this son comes to Me no matter what has gone on throughout the day. Before it's all over for the night, this son looks in My eyes and says, 'Daddy, can I just crawl up on Your lap and sit with You for a few minutes?'" He said, "This son has a relationship built on knowing how much I love him and that no matter what, I long to be with him just as he longs to be with Me. I desire this more than anything else."

I could literally feel His words penetrating the deepest parts of me, and He continued by saying, "And this son is always free to ask anything of Me. He is free to share everything in his heart with Me. This son knows he's My son, and with it, that everything I have is his. It is My pleasure to give him things whenever I feel like it. He holds so much more than he could ever earn—he holds My heart. This son isn't bound by proving he is worthy of an allowance because he knows that everything I have is his *inheritance*."

Then He finished, "My heart is for you to come before Me like your girls come to you; to be like them."

At that point in my "moment" with the Lord, I can recall coming back to the world around me. As a matter of fact, it was as if about thirty minutes of driving happened in an instant, because all I remember of the actual drive is making the final turn toward the pizzeria, about two miles away. I visually cleared the traffic and on the right-hand side, as I crossed railroad tracks in making the right turn, there was a lumberyard I glanced at as my focus turned toward the sky.

Gazing upward I remember an intense feeling of awe and excitement rush over me, and in my mind I pictured the universe literally resting on the Lord's fingertip. At the same time, in what I can only explain as that surreal, yet perfectly reasonable way things happen in a dream, the great God I was seeing had me in His other arm. I said out loud to Him in that moment, "This changes everything."

Change everything it did. This moment with the Lord cemented my identity like nothing I had ever experienced. Almost instantly I was transformed from someone tirelessly working to prove myself into a man who knew exactly where I stood. My whole life up to this point was a mess of feeling undeserving and unworthy, even when I could fake it. I lost years striving to prove to God, my family, friends, and myself that I was capable despite the internal weight that stood to remind me of otherwise. It was miserable never knowing where I truly stood before God and never wanting to know where I really stood before people.

> **It was miserable never knowing where I truly stood before God and never wanting to know where I really stood before people.**

That one exchange with the Lord forever altered my life. No longer did my challenges matter. No longer were my life circumstances an excuse. How could I even care where God placed me, what my "call" was, or which spiritual "gift" was my greatest tool for ministry? God was my Father. God approved of me. As He sustained the universe on His fingertip, He held me in His arms. Life would never again be about what I could do, but rather it was now about who He was and how that changed everything.

Needless to say, despite being poor, despite feeling like I had missed so many opportunities in life, despite knowing my own failures better than anyone else in the world, the last thing I needed from God was a job, or an anointing, or anything else besides Himself. All of the things I would bombard heaven for in prayer, thinking they would solve my problems or answer my questions, were instantly laid to rest. When you discover your place as the beloved child of God, *it changes everything.*

A BOND THICKER THAN BLOOD

Our confidence in this life is Jesus. Our hope in this life is Christ alone. Because the Gospel has vacated our guilt and declared us innocent on account of Christ's sacrifice for us, and because in that same act He promised us eternal life in union with God, we have been declared sons and daughters of God Almighty, so long as we *hold firmly to that hope and confidence.*[107]

You cannot hold firmly to something that is moving while you stand still. Sons and daughters must move forward, they must grow, because in the Kingdom—*the family*—of God, nothing can remain stagnant. There are no birth defects in the Lord's bloodline. Discipleship is the process of us becoming supernaturally adopted and transformed into the spiritual children of God by receiving His life in us, as a part of us, when we turn to follow Jesus.

Reading from the end of Romans 4 we see, "it (righteousness which makes us His children) shall be imputed (placed within us as our possession) into us who believe Jesus Christ." What happens is this:

---

[107] See Hebrews 10.

1. What Jesus did gives us the legal identity as God's children and access to Him and His possessions; it pardons us from being judged unholy and therefore unites us to God.
2. As His children, and during the walk of discipleship, following Jesus changes us so our lives begin to look like the Son's life. We actually learn to interact with the Father and His creation like only His kids can.

Doesn't this make sense? In our learning to live sacrificially and obediently before God, we reveal His fatherly love because we are being shaped by it firsthand. It is actually His pleasure to be a part of our growing up. As much as I want my kids to grow up and be perfectly awesome adults, there is a part of me that wants them to be kids forever. I want to experience every minute of them being babies even when I'm a few diaper explosions into a day. I want to watch my kids learn to walk, even after seeing them trip and split their lips. I want to be at their side when they learn to pedal a bike or swim.

Often we rush the process with the Lord because we desire the "rewards" of maturity, but we don't realize that when we miss out on our identity as His kids we surrender our innocence, growing cold and hard as we "grow up," because at the same time we are learning to *grow alone*. This mindset mistakenly craves usefulness to bring contentment instead of remaining needy and finding satisfaction only in the presence of God. **Blessed are you who hunger now, for you shall be filled.**[108]

By the flesh, such a connection with the Lord is impossible because He is an eternal spirit. Even the flesh's strongest bonds—those of natural family and physical

---

[108] Luke 6:21

blood—are not strong enough to endure in a relationship like that which God desires. Bonds of blood can be broken through pride, lust, and ambition. Even family becomes expendable when the will to survive or the human hunger for power is given free rein in the heart.

It's the outworking of the Gospel that transforms the human heart. Discipleship submits the whole of our person to the presence of God daily by remaining on the cross and learning to find life in the work of Christ alone. As Paul writes in Romans, we submit to Christ in turning away from the world so that our minds become transformed and we can know God's will.[109]

God never intends that we would know something for knowledge's sake. We are to know God's will so that ours is transformed to be His own; and this in order that we can do His will as Jesus did. In this way, we are made more than our human potential and systems allow. Supernaturally, the bonds of this world—physical bonds that will perish with our human bodies one day—are subjected to the Spirit of God. ***My Father will give you whatever you ask in My name.***[110]

When we are led by the Spirit, we actualize our right as children of God; and this by putting to practice what we have been given in Christ. In the outworking of a life surrendered to the leadings of the Spirit, we become more than the sum of human ability and grow into His children; beings truly submitted to the power of the Spirit of God. In this we are bonded together with our Lord and each other, and through an eternal power that is greater than this world.

The bonds of heaven that unite people by the Spirit of God can literally take people, once at enmity with each other and God, and bring them into a union that

---

[109] See Romans 12:2.
[110] Adapted from John 15:16.

can endure the tests of this world and the human heart. Broken people, healed and united in the bond that binds the Godhead together, and displaying the selfless love of God to the world, is the ultimate relational desire of the Father toward us—*His children*, in the earth.

This manifests in all walks of life, no matter our age, and regardless of our "calling." No one is called to be a worker for the Lord who is not first His child. There is not a child of the Lord's outside of His parenting. The sad truth is that there are just as many people working in churches who refuse to listen for, and respond to, the Lord's voice as there are working in pizzerias or post offices. God's plan for this world is that there will be as many missionaries in our grocery stores and public schools as there are in foreign villages or impoverished orphanages. God's plan is for us to be the same people when we wear titles as when wear pajamas—to act the same in a church crowd as we do in a crowded mall.

> **We are to know God's will so that ours is transformed to be His own; and this in order that we can do His will as Jesus did.**

Sonship is the place in which we are established in our eternal connection and covenant to the Lord, and where we learn the Father and His heart for us by experiencing life with Him. Sonship is not just knowing doctrine or practicing religious rite. Sonship is our life in the Father's lap. This happens daily, it happens unrehearsed, and it happens to all who willingly open their heart to the reality of the vastness of His love for them. Sonship is a living dependency on God that is formed in His very arms as we learn that He loves and desires us as His kids, even more than we want Him as our God in our most desperate moments. ***Believe in the light, that you may become sons of light.***[111]

CIRCUMCISION

In the Old Testament, when the Lord called Abraham in order that He could establish a people by which He could reveal Himself to the world, there were certain requirements. Just as the Gospel demands a response, Abraham's calling[112] required he act in consecration to the Lord. If our holy God draws us to Himself as sons and daughters, there will always come with that calling a distinction. We are not called into gray areas with the Lord. When we are called into Him, we are called out of the world.

In Abraham's day, just as it is now, faith was the distinction. Paul made this clear in Romans. However, circumcision was added as a physical act of consecration to the Lord when Abraham faltered in faith and had his son Ishmael, trying in his own strength to accomplish what God had promised. We cannot fulfill the promises of God. He does that. Our task is to stay humble and available. When Abraham tried and failed, God required the most sacred, hidden place of his body to be marked for the Lord. There is no better way to get right to the heart of the matter than to ask a man to take a sword to his manhood.

I sing hallelujah because the fleshly requirement in Abraham's day has been fulfilled in relationship with Christ. Circumcision is for us an act of the heart, in response to the marks on Jesus's body. We are sealed by faith in what Jesus did.[113] In fact, the New Testament apostles clearly

---

[111] Adapted from John 12:36.

[112] See Genesis 12 for Abraham's calling and read through chapter 17 for his circumcision, after he had Ishmael. Note: Abraham was referred to as Abram until God renamed him.

[113] See Romans chapters 3 and 4.

stated that to be a Jew—an identity previously marked by the forefathers with a physical circumcision—was always intended by God to be a circumcision of the heart.

Inasmuch, we are now considered the family of God more so than the Jews were under the law, *if* we live by faith in Jesus as children of God. In fact, the New Testament declares that no matter what our earthly bloodline is, that every person in the world is able to be adopted into the familial covenant of God, which is provided through the grace of Jesus Christ. Ours is the circumcision which cuts us away from the world and the love for it. Paul declared to the Romans:[114]

> "Therefore, if an uncircumcised man keeps the righteous requirements of the law, will not his uncircumcision be counted as circumcision? ...he is a Jew who is one inwardly, and circumcision is that of the heart, in the Spirit, not in the letter; whose praise is not from men, but from God."

In walking with the Lord, sonship is the process of being adopted into the eternal family of God. We become permanent members by the washing and filling of the blood of Jesus and the regeneration which is ours by way of God's own Spirit dwelling in us. In order to be adopted into this new family, we must also renounce our rights to our family of old. As we circumcise our hearts, there is a conscious separation that occurs from anything that is below the bond of our eternal family. It is as if, being citizens of our homeland, we are unable to also identify as citizens of a rogue or enemy nation.

In coming into the eternal family of God as His children, we must be able to see even our birth family as

---

[114] Romans 2:26-29

temporal, and surrender those relationships to the spiritual covenant we have with God. Covenant with God is bound by the blood of Jesus and ratified by God's "gift" to us of His indwelling Spirit.

One of the harshest realities of choosing to walk in this relationship with the Lord is that it will cost us some of our beloved earthly relationships. Not everyone will approve of our spiritual walk or walk with us as we choose to turn from the world toward Jesus. Although I am mentioning this briefly, as the cost of discipleship is repeated many times throughout this book, it must be said that no one caught in a servant's mind-set will be willing to endure the pain and shame of having to make choices at times for Jesus that may result in losing relationship with people we love.

> **Covenant with God is bound by the blood of Jesus and ratified by God's "gift" to us of His indwelling Spirit.**

Remember, when left alone, people are lovers of "self" before anything else, even family members. Sometimes we don't want to believe that, and we use expressions we can see, and through which others can see us, to paint over that innate heart condition. But if you haven't already, there will come a day where you will be rejected for faith in Him, just as Christ said. Only a foundation built on the relationship of children and their perfectly loving eternal Father can endure such things. ***Anyone who loves their father or mother more than Me is not worthy of Me.***[115]

---

[115] Matthew 10:37 (NIV)

THE EVER-INCREASING KINGDOM

Before we leave this chapter I think it is important to take a brief top-down look at sonship in the Word. My ultimate purpose is not to give you theological tools so you can say you understand more of the Bible and become satisfied. My desire is to create avenues through which you can press deeper into relationship with the Lord and by which you can grow in experience and intimacy with His heart. There are some things I feel are important to at least look at in the big picture so as to glean a bit of His heart, and to encourage you when moments of coming to Him may feel like a labor; when intimacy seems hard to come by. ***The one who stands firm to the end will be saved.***[116]

At the beginning people were created in the perfection of Eden and given all we needed to dwell in mutual space with God Himself. The moment that place was violated in Adam and Eve's unfaithfulness and pride, sin entered their lives and in mercy they were cast out of God's presence. Had they remained there, they would have died eternally, or been instantly destroyed as rebels to God's holiness. The temporal cannot remain in the presence of the eternal because, by definition, their nature separates them. God understood this before creation.

The Word tells us that redemption was His plan before the world was formed.[117] The distinction of creation, as below the Creator, was necessary in order for that creation to eventually be united with God in eternity—beyond the boundaries of the Garden. So Jesus actually died the moment creation became God's intention. If God would pay for our sin with His own life, we could then be given

---

[116] Matthew 10:22 (NIV)
[117] See 1 Peter 1:18-21.

the value and nature of God without violating the very things that make Him God: eternity and perfection.

In this exchange God did something remarkable. Rather than simply award us a ticket to heaven, God gave us new identity as His children. God was willing to give Jesus as the payment for us to be with Him. Therefore, the "ticket" we get to eternity with Him is the identity, right, and inheritance of *the One* who died and was raised for us.

You see, God has spoken to us about His intention for our eternity together. Many think we will arrive one day in heaven and enter an eternity-long worship service led by saints and angels. Thank the Lord that is not the case. Even if heaven has an endless supply of good coffee and bagels, I cannot imagine enduring a worship set list I would ever want to continue in forever. Neither can God.

> **The mark of God's children is their obedience to the Spirit.**

His plan is that we would join Him in heaven and stand with His firstborn Son in the revealing of God's glory forever. He wants us to join Him and Jesus in eternal creation, life, and the fellowship of peace and joy in the family of God. Even more, it is His design that we begin practicing this here and now, in this earthly life.

Scripture testifies to the specific dynamic that exists between a father and son. That is the relationship which God has designed to be the foundation on which He redeems the world and receives the world as His own. It is from this fatherly position that God rules the world with the love and justice of heaven. Paul says in Romans that all of creation is frustrated and waits for the children of God to be revealed so that God's order can be restored and life in God returned to the world.[118]

If, as Paul says in Romans and Galatians, the mark of God's children is their obedience to the Spirit of God, then it is understandable how God reveals Himself through us—His Spirit's power, love, and nature get shown to the world by His kids being like Jesus. Disciples reveal the one they follow. ***The glory which You gave Me, I have given them.***

Paul also explains, as does the writer of Hebrews, that as far back as the Old Testament covenant with Abraham and Israel, God's intention was to make a people His children in the earth.[119] This happens not because people are Jews or of a certain earthly descent, but because faith in God to redeem us through Jesus is where grace becomes our possession and a person becomes God's spiritual (or eternal) child.

Prophets throughout biblical history declared that God would first raise up the Son, and then many sons and daughters would follow, by which God would build "an ever-increasing Kingdom" and administer justice to all the world.[120] The prophets declared that the Son of God would inherit the nations (and in essence, gain people of all descent) as His own, whereby He would bring them into adoption as children of God.[121]

Understanding this really is a lot simpler than a theological study. That a Father would desire sons and daughters over servants to carry on His legacy and to join Him in His eternal purpose is simply the natural product of familial love. Sons (and daughters) can become who their heavenly

---

[118] See Romans 8:19-21.
[119] Paul writes of these things in Romans (see chapter 8), Galatians (see chapters 3:26-4:7), and Hebrews speaks on this in chapter 2:10-18.
[120] See Isaiah 9.
[121] See Psalm 2.

Father is because they actually possess a part of His being. Children have an inherent interest in the Father's interests. At best, servants can only learn to do what their sovereign master does, acquire from Him what they earn, and even if they treat the master's interests as their own, will never possess His identity outside of adoption.[122]

Sonship is the establishment of a relationship built upon the work of the Gospel that reveals the tenderness, care, long-suffering, and love of our Father. When this is forged in our souls, we are brought to the place in relationship where disciples of Jesus go from the understanding of a servant's promotion for good service to the reality of inheriting all that the Father will ever have simply because He loves them.

God has chosen this as the way He will bring heaven to earth. Literally, the Word declares that the Lord will establish His Kingdom through His Son and enforce His dominion through the raising up of His sons and daughters in the earth. Truly this is an otherworldly task for us as mere human beings. However, having been empowered by His love and care for us, we can walk with the confidence of being the children of God. ***For nothing is impossible with God.***[123]

> But to all who believed Him and accepted Him,
> He gave the right to become children of God.
> They are reborn—not with a physical birth
> resulting from human passion or plan,
> but a birth that comes from God.
>
> —John 1:12,13 (NLT)

---

[122] Refer to Jesus's words in John 10 for more on this.
[123] Luke 1:37 (NLT)

5

BROKENNESS

BROKENNESS: AN INVITATION
by Janet Mwinilamba Hart
Faithful Wife and Mother
Co-Founding Pastor, Church of New Life for All Nations,
Livingstone, Zambia
A pillar of brokenness

My journey into brokenness is one of humility and obedience to the conviction of the Word and the Holy Spirit of God. I speak of a life of dying to self, my own interests, comfort, and laying down all for Christ's sake; an absolute surrender of my will to the will of God. Daily I live in the Potter's hands, being molded and walking in discipline according to God's Word.

I have learned that brokenness is not just an emotion, but also an act of the will. "Not my will Lord, but yours...." When I look to the life of Jesus, I see that He totally submitted to the will of the Father God (Luke 22:42) when He was faced with the cup of suffering. A journey of brokenness is not an easy road, but when you know the Word of God and the benefits thereof, you cannot afford *not* to live in brokenness.

In 1996, when my husband, David Irving Hart died, I was faced with a situation that needed a drastic and immediate decision concerning ministry. David, an American from Connecticut, yielded to God's call to go and start the Church of New Life for All Nations in Livingstone, Zambia. Our passion was evangelism and discipleship. On March 9, 1996, David died from blackwater fever. We buried his body on Thursday, and that same day the Lord spoke to me to preach on Sunday.

Now traditionally as a Zambian, it's not right to preach when you have just lost a loved one. At the same time, I knew that esteeming the tradition of man above the will of the Spirit makes the Word of God of no effect, as displayed in Mark 7. Clearly, I heard God saying to preach, but I argued with Him, saying to the Lord, "What will people say and think for me to stand at the pulpit just a few days after burial?"

The Lord spoke again, saying, "You either preach, or never will."

That Sunday I preached a message titled, "How to Stand in the Midst of a Crisis." It was at this point I truly learned humility, obedience, and sacrifice. It was then I learned how to be broken and surrender my will to God, stripping of self-reliance and having total dependence on God. You must understand that brokenness is not a show of weakness, *per se*, but of strength. James 4:6 (ESV) says, "God opposes the proud, but gives grace to the humble." Verse 10 (NIV) says, "Humble yourself before the Lord, and He will lift you up."

See, we are in an age where most stewards of God have gotten off track by allowing title, fame, and the profit of prosperity messages to override the message of brokenness, the cross, repentance, and holiness. There are so many laid-back attitudes and deceptions in the church now, more than ever before. My cry is to see the Body of Christ get back to seeking Him and hungering for God's Word, which is truth and life.

There is something about reaching a breaking point, or a crisis, that causes one to seek God more earnestly, especially when you are walking in the truth of God's Word. Psalm 34:17,18 (NIV) reads, "The righteous cry out, and the Lord hears them; he delivers them from all their troubles. The Lord is close to the brokenhearted, and saves those who are crushed in spirit."

Brokenness carried me through the years of challenges I faced in life and ministry after my husband died. I faced rejection from those I thought stood with us, church splits by those I raised in our own home, was financially plundered by those that I had helped, and was falsely accused of things I did not say or do. People looked for ways to annoy and offend me. Yet, in all of this, I learned not to defend myself, but to be the one who would apologize.

I always remembered my husband's words, "Jesus went to the cross for something He did not do." It was brokenness that made our Lord Jesus of no reputation. I paraphrase Philippians 2:7 in saying, "Jesus did not seek fame or honor." *Jesus forgave* those who ridiculed or denied Him. With this great example, I too decided to die to self; to love and forgive.

This is not an easy road with the help of the Holy Spirit. It is impossible without Him.

In brokenness, as according to Isaiah 57:15, it is the spirit of the humble and contrite heart which is revived. This is the secret key to unlocking God's promises in my life. My life of faith and dependence on God has brought me divine provision in different ways. It has taken me to preach the Gospel in different nations of the world. When you live in brokenness, you live a sacrificial life, yielding to

> **This is not an easy road with the help of the Holy Spirit. It is impossible without Him.**

God's Word, and this leads you to a life of spiritual maturity. This involves perseverance and discipline, regardless of the fierce battles you will face.

I now end with saying, just as Paul said in Galatians 2:20 (NASB): "I have been crucified with Christ. It is no longer I who live, but Christ who lives in me. And the life I now live in the flesh I live by faith in the Son of God, who loved me and gave Himself for me."

Can you also say the same as Paul said, or are you still looking for a way to get there? Isaiah chapter 35:8 (NASB) says, "A highway will be there, a roadway, and it will be called the *Highway of Holiness*; the unclean shall not pass over it. It shall belong to those who walk in the way...." *Whoever* walks the road, although a fool, shall not go astray. May you be among the *whoever* that is broken, to walk the broken road.

* * *

JARS OF CLAY

No one likes getting hurt. Yet flinching is not an inherent human instinct. Flinching is one of our earliest learned behaviors. Interestingly, the fear of falling is, however, a natural human instinct with which every child is born. Human beings come into this world, despite not being able to do anything more than cry and flail helplessly, and we know these two things: that God has not given us a spirit of fear;[124] and that we were not created to fall.[125]

Once again, we are caught in the murkiness between the innocence of childhood and the intended destiny for

---

[124] 2 Timothy 1:7
[125] Isaiah 43:7 says all of God's children were created for GLORY, not failure.

glory for which God has designed us. We enter this world much like Adam and Eve; blank and at the point most easily connected to God. We arrive without specific sin yet with the desire to be autonomous lying in wait somewhere within us, calling us to prove ourselves to God by choosing independence.

Independence leads to separation from His presence. Like a baby, our instinct knows He is there despite knowing nothing else. We are born with a confidence in our parents; it's our instinctual knowledge that He holds us and won't let us fall. Yet the human drive to grow up leads us to try and be our own god and takes us off of the destiny God designed, that we would one day be glorified with Him. We find ourselves again needing to know two things: who God is, and what the implications of that knowledge are.

> **As the Lord redeems the brokenness we experience as His children, the reality is that there is nowhere we can go in this life where He is absent.**

Brokenness is the place where we are reshaped and reformed to contain more than just a glimpse of the Lord. It is not enough for us to have a dormant instinct that testifies of God within us, as a baby who is without any strength or experience to test and season the instinct. We must have practice with that instinct, translating it into a voluntary expression that is as natural to us as reacting to love with a smile. As the Lord redeems the brokenness we experience as His children, the reality is that there is nowhere we can go in this life where He is absent.

We learn that there is no situation that He has not covered and that the fear of adversity is ultimately more dangerous than the adversity itself. That's because death—our greatest enemy—has already been defeated. As David learned, *though we walk through the valley of the shadow of death we have to fear no evil, for God is with us and He comforts us in His strength with His presence.*[126] When you have survived your own brokenness and seen yourself as a broken vessel, redeemed and polished by the very hand of God, you become a willing instrument at God's disposal, always available to reveal Him. You even learn that there is joy in the process.

> **In the Potter's hand is the only place the pot has no fear of being broken, for in the Potter's hand will always rise a greater vessel.**

In the Potter's hand is the only place the pot has no fear of being broken, for in the Potter's hand will always rise a greater vessel.

Maybe now you can understand why I said earlier that there was no way forward with the Lord until you encounter the endless love of the Father. Who else can you trust to walk you through brokenness? Who in the universe could you expect to endure with you as you face the toughest places in life and confront the emptiest places in yourself, beyond the Father who created you and who wants to see you succeed more than anyone else in the world?

The truth is, if you do not share a relationship with God in which you know Him as "Daddy," I am not convinced you could ever have the confidence to hang on for the ride when it takes you right to your breaking. Unless you come to know the joy and satisfaction of your heavenly Daddy's love and affection, I don't believe there is anything else that can teach you to fall in love with those people who will

---

[126] Adapted from Psalm 23.

help usher in your breaking; to view them the same way Christ did those who nailed Him to the cross.

There is simply no other way than the one bloody road of brokenness. The discipleship road leads to simultaneously experiencing the power of a God-filled life while being humbled to express that power selflessly as Christ has done for us. ***That the love with which You loved Me may be in them....***[127]

PRESSED ON EVERY SIDE

"This will be the last night we sit like this together."[128]

For some time now everyone in the room had the sense that this Passover would be unlike any they had ever before experienced. In each of their hearts His words had been planted for some three years now. Across all of Judea they had walked with Him, and by now they'd seen things they never dreamed possible become normal. And there, in a common upper room, they gathered like they had every year of their lives before, to honor God's mercy toward them and their forefathers.

Yet this Passover came with the sense that His words spoke about something more than they could fathom. It all seemed to be building, all of the sermons and miracles, all of the private lessons and challenges. All of the quiet times they shared and meals they ate seemed to have orchestrated this one moment. As the evening deepened into night, the familiar smell of tradition mixed with burning lamp oil could only offer a comfort that they all somehow knew His words were threatening to shatter.

---

[127] From John 17:26.

[128] This story was rendered from the Gospel accounts of the "Last Supper"; see Matthew 26, Mark 14, Luke 22, and John 13.

"The one whose hand is in the cup with Mine has already betrayed Me." Jesus always spoke in parables, but this felt different. Sure enough, Judas's eyes fixed on Him as if he knew precisely what Jesus was saying. "What you are doing," Jesus continued, as He looked back at the one named Iscariot, "do it quickly."

Before anyone knew what to do, Judas collected himself and left the room. All eyes were back on the Teacher. They were unsure, but that hadn't changed for years now. Only now they were learning to remain steady, so long as Jesus was with them.

As that breath left His lips, deafening silence filled the room.

And then He uttered, "Fear not. This was ordered from above. The time has come for Me to leave you." His voice was different tonight. It was as if every moment of the last three years, every emotion and every demonstration, was being mixed and compounded into each steady word. They could feel every letter. "It is time for Me to finish My work. They will come for Me soon."

As that breath left His lips, deafening silence filled the room. In that moment, no one knew what to do. Some glanced at Peter, having gotten used to his brash reactions, hoping he'd have something to say this time that might actually move the Lord to a different end. But Peter held his tongue, at least for now.

After the longest half-minute they'd yet endured together, Jesus broke the unease, "The Son of Man has glorified God, and now is the time for God to glorify His Son." Jesus anguished over these words. Maybe only the day He stood before Lazarus's tomb could anyone compare to what they were seeing in Him now. "But He will also now glorify Himself."

It seemed as if the Teacher was drifting back into parables, but each of them knew this was not simply a lesson. They could feel the Lord's heart pouring over them in the words He spoke. Just moments before He had washed their feet. They were honored and joyed after He made their soles clean. But the sober urgency with which He did so had foretold of the trembling their inner souls were feeling now.

Jesus continued, "My children, I will only be with you a little longer. And you will seek Me, but you cannot come to the place I will go. It is important you hang on to this new commandment: Love one another just as I have loved you. By this all will know that you are Mine." The disciples in the room exchanged glances. Somehow they sensed in His words that they would soon be all each other had left in this world.

Peter couldn't hold back any longer, "Lord, where is it You are going? Why can't I follow You now? I will lay down my life for You!" Each of them could see in Peter their own fear and sadness. This wasn't the Simon Peter always trying to prove himself before Jesus; the guy always shouting to show off what they all knew was at best a tenuous confidence. Like the rest of them, Peter felt the finality of the Lord's words that night, and just as much as he was swearing his allegiance to his Messiah, he was making a plea for the life of the only friend who'd ever loved him as deeply as Jesus did.

"Simon Peter, you don't even know what you say. Would you really die for Me? I promise you, My friend, that before the rooster crows, three times you will deny you even know Me," Jesus replied.

* * *

Most of us know this story.[129] In fact, even if you have never heard it, you know the story. That's because every one of us has come to the place where we have let someone down. In this case, Peter goes on to do exactly as Jesus foretold. After Jesus shows Himself, Moses, and Elijah in glory to Peter, James, and John, Peter still denies having known Him. After having his feet washed by Jesus and being warned of his own looming betrayal, Peter doesn't stay close to his friends for support, or even go seek refuge away from any opportunity to fail.

Brokenness is a place in Christ we must never leave.

After years of seeing this Jesus do the impossible and being at His right hand much of the time; after watching Jesus feed the thousands, after seeing all of the healings and miracles, after bearing witness to the demons fleeing, no—not even after literally walking on raging waters together with Jesus—did Peter have what it took to be faithful in the greatest moment of trial.

Like Peter, most of us have stories of moments where we found out that we were not even close to being who we thought we were. And if you cannot relate to what I am saying, then it is only a matter of time until you discover that you don't have what it takes to be someone worth the life of another, let alone the life of the Savior of the world.

This is the place called brokenness. Before we come through it, the prospect of brokenness casts a terrible pall. Once we get there, brokenness is a place in Christ we must never leave. Brokenness is the place in Christ of our greatest victory, and the place the sons of God drink the cup of suffering in order that the cup would then be filled

---

[129] Adapted from the Gospel accounts of the Last Supper; see Matthew 26, Mark 14, Luke 22, and John 13.

with the glorious heart of God, for the benefit of unworthy humanity.

Brokenness is not a place the Lord commands us to go in order that we be punished for falling short. Brokenness is the place all of us go in this lifetime simply because this world is *broken*. Because of redemption, the place we are broken and where we run out, where we become acquainted with the depth of our weakness, is exactly where we must go to discover the "joy set before Him"[130] which drove Jesus to press on for you and me.

Some will go by loss. Some will go by failure. Still some will go on to be broken by people they love, by circumstance, or by the frustration of waiting. There are those who will be broken just by walking with the Lord. Yes, walking with God breaks the greatest of us. And it's not even His wrath, but it is His very goodness, and His awesome greatness, by which all of us will eventually break. You can only stand by something so immense, by someone so selflessly loving, for so long before the very foundations of who and what you are get reduced to nothing.

Some will go by loss. Some will go by failure. Still some will go on to be broken by people they love, by circumstance, or by the frustration of waiting.

The question is, will we trust God—the God who allowed Jesus to be broken for us—and who, after the breaking, raised Him up in glory, to do the same on our behalf? Will we fashion for ourselves a way out? Many a man or woman have left the cross, deceived into believing that brokenness is supposed to end. Please, hang on for just a little while longer. I beg you, if you are unsure as you read

---

[130] See Hebrews 12:2.

this of where you stand before the Lord, the message of this chapter may be the most important the Lord has ever allowed me to carry. ***Unless you eat the flesh of the Son of Man, and drink His blood, you have no life in you.***[131]

How you respond to brokenness, whether in fear and bitterness, or be it in surrender and finding intimacy before the Lord, may be the most critical dynamic in whether or not you discover true joy in life.

CRUSHED BUT NOT DESTROYED

Just look to Peter and the first disciples once again. After Jesus was crucified, and even after the resurrection, the biblical accounts clearly depict that it was a confusing time for them. They were together, but quite possibly only because there was nowhere else for them to go. No one wanted to be seen with them. In fact, they feared more than just rejection. Jesus was hanged. Not just beaten, no; He wasn't just punished and cast out. Jesus was defiled on a pagan cross. And now so many of the things He had told them of before had come to pass, yet still none of it made sense. There was no power. Where was the Kingdom that Jesus spoke about and even demonstrated?

Things were back to the way they were before Jesus, with the exception that the temple leaders felt more empowered than ever, and Peter and his friends were on the outside looking in for the first time in their lives. Everything they had left their lives for—the One they had been willing to drop everything for and follow—was gone.

Undoubtedly, every one of them now questioned the last three years of their lives. They all must have wrestled with fear and resentment. Surely they were as disappointed in themselves as they were in Jesus. No one knew what

---

[131] John 6:53 (NIV)

the future held. They weren't Romans, and Jews would never receive them again. But who could even go back? How could you go back from the things they saw with Jesus to the dead traditions of the temple, to the bickering and pandering of the elders? The only place these fishermen could go back to was their nets.[132] If the marketplace didn't treat them well at least they'd eat; if they could catch anything, that was.

Then Jesus showed up on the shore of the lake where they were fishing. Like it was with the disciples on the Road to Emmaus, no one could even tell it was Him; at least not until the Lord did something John immediately recognized. Jesus called something that wasn't as if it was. After the futility of striving in their own power, only to be found lacking once again, Jesus compassionately and intentionally called out to their emptiness, "Children, have you any food?"

"No," they answered.

"Cast your net on the other side of the boat, and you will find some," Jesus replied. Then, Scripture tells us, with those words, Jesus filled their nets to the point of breaking as they indulged His request. Yes, that was the picture of the breaking which is caused by generosity being served to the unworthy.

You see, all of us are on a journey with the Lord. Just as the first Disciples, we, as disciples, are each a part of a corporate doing by which God is orchestrating the events of this age to reveal His goodness and to perfect His creation. But at the same time He is walking with each of us individually, taking us personally to places in Him that invigorate us, try us, purify us, and then empower us. Then He does it all over again, but deeper. Deeper, and *deeper still*, is the endless pattern of walking with an endless God. The

---

[132] Refer to John 21 for the complete biblical account.

deeper we break, the greater we are stretched, the larger the vessel that is reformed, and the more of Him we are able to bear. ***I have much more to say to you, more than you can now bear.***[133]

With Peter, as I am sure it was for the other disciples as well, that day on the shore was a turning point that changed the course of history. Peter has gone so low, failing at what was the most critical hour of testing and in the most overwhelming of ways; *barring having nailed Jesus to the cross himself.* Peter could not have possibly felt less capable or undeserving to be called one on which Jesus said, "I will build my church, and the gates of hell will not prevail against it."[134] But Jesus had said those exact words knowing that Peter would later break under pressure. Still, amidst the worst of Peter being laid bare, Jesus never skipped a beat. What the Lord did next is quite possibly my favorite of all the Bible's account of Jesus's doings.

After feeding the hungry disciples breakfast on the shore, for the fishermen had been on the water all night, Jesus turns to Peter and asks him, "Simon Peter, son of Jonah, do you love Me more than these?" Now, it is important to consider Jesus addresses Peter by the name he had when Jesus first called him—Simon son of Jonah, *not* Peter child of God—as if to let Peter know that Jesus was well aware of Peter's failure and the internal unworthiness he must have felt sitting there before the Lord. But remember in your brokenness, if Jesus reminds you to look on your shame, it is not to condemn you, but only to magnify the mercy available to you by His grace.

Moving deeper into the text, we cannot miss that in the original Greek writing, the verse above used the word we know as "agape," which we see translated as the word

---

[133] John 16:12 (NIV)
[134] Matthew 16:18 (NIV)

love. Agape is selfless God-love which dies for another, wanting nothing in return. What is Peter's response to this? How could you even find something to say in that moment when Peter replied, "Yes, Lord, You know that I love You." However, all Peter can summon is the word closest to brotherly love, "philia" as we would see it.

Have you ever disappointed someone so deeply that even when they forgave you, even when they allowed you back in their life and blessed you by doing something like cooking you a meal, it was painfully embarrassing to tell them you loved them in the aftermath of how you had just violated them?

To me, this place is too real. I have been there with the Lord. I have been to a place in my walk with Him where after He saved me, after He healed and restored me, and after He blessed me with the beauty and privilege I have in my family and earthly success, I found my faith and trust in Him utterly bankrupt. And, like Peter, I have heard the Lord's response to me in that moment, "Feed My lambs."

> **But remember in your brokenness, if Jesus reminds you to look on your shame, it is not to condemn you, but only to magnify the mercy available to you by His grace.**

That's right, in spite of being disqualified even after accepting the call and receiving the honor of a disciple, Jesus's response to us is as it was to Peter. In essence, *take care of My children.* Let the floodgates open wide. Jesus trusts Peter *the betrayer* with His kids. This is beyond comprehension.

Jesus doesn't stop there either. Please, if you are able to, read the account in your Bible before you go on. Read the gospel of John, chapter 21, verses 15-19. You will see two more times Jesus asks Peter the same question. What you will not see is that in the Greek text the word Jesus used for love changes each time.

Jesus poses the question a second time with a new word, *eros*, which means intimate love in the Greek. Once again Peter responds affirming Jesus with only the brotherly love he has, love that has already betrayed God's selfless love, and even fails the test of intimate love. Again Jesus answers, "Feed My sheep," or, *take care of My children*. A third time Jesus asked the same question, finally using the same word for love as Peter. It is one more gesture of the Lord's humility in love to all of humanity.

Put yourself in Peter's shoes. He knew he was not able to offer Jesus anything more than brotherly love, and Jesus who just died for Peter, meets Peter where he's at. With his third response, it's as if Peter pleads with Jesus, "Lord, You know all things." *Lord, You know my love is limited. You know that I'm only capable of so much. What more can I say?*

In absolutely unbearable goodness to those that are broken—those who by surrender or crushing have lost the will to even fight for their identity—the Lord says, *I know that I am capable, and I know that you are Mine. Now tend to My children.*

Now you know your own weakness.
Now you understand My love.
Now you can trust in Me.
Now you are broken.
Now I send you to feed My children.

THE ROAD LESS TRAVELED

One of the instincts of human nature is that we generally turn and run from brokenness. We fear our own destruction, and the human spirit that seeks independence cannot rely on its own ability to salvage life from a situation in which they already created death. So we rationalize, we compare, we reduce, and we justify in order to convince ourselves that we aren't really broken—we're just leaky. We're just a little loose and we just need a tune-up. In his timeless book, *The Pursuit of God*, A.W. Tozer writes,

> "In the world of men we find nothing approaching the virtues of which Jesus spoke in the opening words of the famous Sermon on the Mount. Instead of poverty of spirit we find the rankest kind of pride; instead of mourners we find pleasure seekers; instead of meekness, arrogance; instead of hunger after righteousness we hear men saying, 'I am rich and increased with goods and have need of nothing'; instead of mercy we find cruelty; instead of purity of heart, corrupt imaginings; instead of peacemakers we find men quarrelsome and resentful; instead of rejoicing in most treatment we find them fighting back with every weapon at their command.
>
> Of this kind of moral stuff civilized society is composed. The atmosphere is charged with it; we breathe it with every breath and drink it with our mother's milk. Culture and education refine these things slightly but leave them basically untouched."[135]

Truer words than these may have never been penned in this regard. We believe that if we move the bandages onto the most recently bleeding wounds that there won't be a larger systemic problem. But that returns us to one of our earliest points of discussion. *We are broken.* We come to the Gospel broken, we come to our Daddy broken, and as long as we carry our stinking robes of flesh, we are undeniably broken. And around again we come to one word that answers it all: REDEMPTION.

---

[135] A.W. Tozer, *The Pursuit of God* (Harrisburg, PA: Christian Publications, Inc.), Kindle edition.

Through the ransom Jesus paid and the provision He has made, the Father doesn't punish brokenness; He injects Himself into it and brings life where life is otherwise impossible. He is the only lasting value we will ever find in ourselves, and in being and remaining broken before the Lord we are positioned to always expect more of Him to fill and flow through us. *I will give you rest.*[136]

Sadly, we often reduce brokenness to moments or lessons that can be "overcome," and in doing so, we never actually reap the benefits that experiencing brokenness with Christ can produce in us. There is no place in the Christian life where more people get sidetracked and leave the road with Christ. In the years I have known Christ and His Church, I have seen people get more creative in avoiding places of spiritual breaking and stripping than just about anything else. It is actually part of the greater human condition whereby we see only "as the flesh sees." We must exchange a short-term temporal view of our walk with Christ for the eternal view He desires us to have.

Entire worldviews, governments, cultures, and even ministries have arisen out of the human struggle to relieve or prevent brokenness. But think this all the way through. If Jesus didn't excuse Himself from brokenness or choose another path to glory, then how can we believe in doctrines or systems that promise us as much? A person who has "passed the test" of brokenness and no longer needs to stay there is a person learning to take credit for their success and unwittingly paying into future failure. Leaving the place of brokenness is the fastest way to see the glory of God depart.

"Blessed are the poor in spirit, for theirs is the kingdom of heaven.... Blessed are the pure in heart, for they shall see God."[137] These words of Jesus are as true now as the

---

[136] Matthew 11:28 (NIV)
[137] Matthew 5:3,8

moment the Lord spoke them. Just as Tozer implied, humanity resists brokenness in all of its doings. The danger in this is not in protecting ourselves, but in actually resisting God. If God is manifest where purity exists, then purity can be found where poverty of spirit is. Maybe remaining on the cross—remaining broken—*carrying our cross,* as Jesus said, really is the best place for us to be. Brokenness sanctifies. Brokenness that is redeemed by the Lord begets a people whose hearts are positioned to see God.

> **Brokenness that is redeemed by the Lord begets a people whose hearts are positioned to see God.**

We would be missing something if the word discipline wasn't mentioned here. There is great debate over what exactly discipline is in regards to the Lord. Even when we can agree with Scripture which says, "the Lord disciplines the one He loves,"[138] our prideful resistance to submission and our fear of rejection often pervert our view of God's discipline. But remember, Jesus told the disciples that if "people know how to give good gifts to your children, how much more will your heavenly Father give good gifts…?" James wrote that "every perfect gift is from above, coming down from the Father of lights with whom there is no variation or shadow due to change."[139]

Now look, if we rightly respond to the Gospel, the discipline of the Lord is unquestionably good. If He really is a good Father who gives good things and never changes, if He paid with Jesus's life so we could be adopted, and if God the Father has truly positioned Himself toward us in love and bent the universe to make way for our redemption,

---

[138] Hebrews 12:6 (NLT)
[139] James 1:17 (ESV)

then what can we possibly fear in His discipline? First John 4:17,18 reveals the heart of the issue:

> By this love is perfected with us, so that we may have confidence for the day of judgment, because as he is so are we in this world. There is no fear in love, but perfect love casts out fear. For fear has to do with punishment, and whoever fears has not been perfected in love (ESV).

In this verse, John points out a few key issues. First, the terms of love are laid out for us: God has selflessly given Himself to us in order that we can face judgment with the confidence that we will not be destroyed. Then, he explains that perfect love doesn't include fear because God's children are not facing punishment; we know that we only face redemption and union. John finishes by saying that when fear is present, love still has not been perfected.

We resist discipline and correction the same way we oppose brokenness. But discipline and correction are ways in which God fixes brokenness, be it the brokenness of a momentary disobedience, or that of long-term defiance which the Lord wants to guide into humble responsiveness to Him. God's discipline is meant for our closeness to Him, that things which cannot stand in His presence be addressed and exchanged for eternal things. This is where you can pick it back up in Hebrews and read chapter 12, verses 5-11.

God is treating us as His children when He disciplines us, "for it yields the peaceful fruit of righteousness to those who have been trained by it." If we refuse discipline because we fear being exposed, rejected, or punished, then we have accepted our own pride which declares we don't need God's help, refused to live in the faith that He is good, or denied that the work of Christ was complete.

We all want God to show up in our lives. There are so many situations where we need Him, where we long for Him, and yet we resist taking the one position which ushers His heart into our circumstance. God gives grace to the humble. Why is it that we resist getting low before Him? Even when we muster up the strength to humble ourselves, so often we do it simply as a token, to pay the bill so we will then have some sort of leverage to ask—no, demand—that God raise us up to the place of status we covet. We are always searching for ways to work our will into situations.

> **There are so many situations where we need Him, and yet we resist taking the one position which ushers His heart into our circumstance.**

You see, you cannot both come to God with a clear conscience and be willing for Him to take you anywhere and through anything, *for His glory*, while also holding on to the expectation for it to happen the way you want it or when you want it. That's playing both sides. The expectation is that God will show up. Rest is found in His goodness and ability. The example is always Jesus Christ, who was glorified after carrying the cross, hanging on the cross, and ascending from the cross with scars on His back and holes in His hands. ***I am the resurrection and the life.***[140]

That's right, even now Jesus both carries His brokenness and is eternally glorified. He was a marked man who now *marks men*. As He suffers in pursuit of those who are lost, interceding before the Father for their very souls,[141] He is also displaying and expressing all the Father's glory in order that the lost be brought in. And He does this through

---

[140] See John 11:25.
[141] See Hebrews 7:25.

us. Paul wrote to the Romans[142] that as God's children we jointly inherit all that Christ has, "if indeed we suffer with Him, that we also may be glorified together."

FREE INDEED

Where do we find hope when we discover our brokenness cannot be fixed in our own strength? Our hope is in the power of salvation which raised Christ from the dead and has been offered to us in the Gospel. What is it that continues to point and beckon us to walk in brokenness? The call Jesus Christ has made to discipleship takes us only down one road. What is it that holds us and keeps us in the most difficult and deepest places of breaking? The intimate love we share with our Father is the very confidence we can have that in being broken, we will not be destroyed.

Why is it that brokenness has been ordained as the crucible for perfect union with the Lord and His saints? Because only in being broken of our self, cast utterly into desperate reliance on His Spirit, and clothed in the humility of the crucified Jesus, can we truly discover freedom in this life. As Paul wrote, "It is for freedom Christ has set us free."[143] In other words, there is but one goal for which Christ has liberated us: that as God first created us, so we shall be restored to freedom in order that others will be loosed. So has He loosed us from the curse of death; *just as God is, so shall we be free.*

How can one be free when Christ's own words call us slaves?

How can one be free when Christ's own words call us slaves to the Lord; when Paul calls us bondservants of love or

---

[142] See Romans 8:14-17.
[143] See Galatians 5:1.

slaves of righteousness? How can we, though being "slaves, live as the Lord's freedmen," as Paul writes in 1 Corinthians 7:21? Because the freedom designed for the disciples of Christ is freedom from our "self." Left alone, "self" always leads us into the eternal bondage of sin and broken relationship with God. Crushed and redeemed, the "self" is purged to create the place in us which Christ inhabits.

If we are to be filled by His Spirit—in order that we would be perfectly fitted together with the Lord and can manifest the image and likeness of Jesus—then we must first be broken of our self-will, self-service, and self-image. It is better for us to be crushed by the hand of the living God in order that we can be redeemed and restored by His love than to remain unbroken and suffer a life of stubbornly refusing intimacy with Him.

Remember John the Baptist, who cried out, "He must increase, but I must decrease."[144] Or let us live by the apostle Paul's decree, "It is no longer I who live, but Christ lives in me."[145] Even Job, the Old Testament example, who lived without the testimony of the Holy Spirit dwelling in people because the Gospel had not yet been made manifest to mankind through Jesus, cried out saying, "Though God might kill me, my hope is only in Him."[146]

Just as living in continual death on the cross is actually a gift of life which positions us to continuously see resurrection, so is a life of brokenness before God and men the only place in which we are positioned to be more than just gifted people doing powerfully supernatural things. Sure, it might be cool to be the gifted guy or girl in the room, but Christ isn't interested in that—He desires those who will pay the price to share the Father's nature.

---

[144] John 3:30
[145] Galatians 2:20
[146] See Job 13:15.

Brokenness is the heart position of the sons and daughters of God bowed before the Father in humility and service to all He loves. When you are laid low before the Lord and yet experience His loving endorsement, there is nothing in this world to fear; no reason to defend or protect what God has validated. In the end, brokenness isn't an experience or moment that we need to overcome, but a position of humility we must take up before God and man by which true freedom is expressed. ***If the Son makes you free, you shall be free indeed.***[147]

This freedom is key in the life of a believer, of a son or daughter, who is called as an ambassador of heaven to the earth. In 1 Corinthians chapters 12 and 13, the apostle Paul writes of all of the spiritual gifts given to the Body of Christ for the church's edification. In chapter 13, he sums them all up by saying, though he may have all of the gifts, "but have not love, it profits me nothing."

Paul then goes on to tell of the selfless nature of love. He tells us that love, "suffers long and is kind…does not envy…parade itself, is not puffed up…does not seek its own…thinks no evil…[love] bears all things, believes all things, hopes all things, endures all things." Then, he declares, "Love never fails…prophecies, they will fail…tongues, they will fail…knowledge, it will vanish."

In order that we can be positioned like this before each other and the world, our self-will and the "pride of life" must be, and stay, broken. How else can we truly live, as Paul says in his second letter to the Corinthians, *compelled* by the love of God? In this way he writes, "From now on, we regard no one according to the flesh…if anyone is in Christ, he is a new creation." Only the eyes of a broken man or woman can stay in focus by love, always viewing

---

[147] John 8:36

others—no matter how they view or treat us—with the potential of heaven.

One who is broken and submitted to the Spirit will see all of creation as redeemable through the Spirit's eyes. One who is broken before the Lord and men, because of their standing in the identity and approval of the immovable God, is the one who can truly live. As Paul proclaimed, one who has been "reconciled to God Himself, through Jesus Christ,"[148] and who has "the ministry of reconciliation";[149] is one of God's children upon the earth who act in His stead as an "ambassador for Christ."[150] This walking in love, by Paul's account, is *a more excellent way*[151] even than walking in the gifts of church position and demonstrating of the supernatural.

> **One who is broken and submitted to the Spirit will see all of creation as redeemable.**

DIVERSIONS

Once again, I remind you that my intention through this book is not to tell you how to accomplish discipleship. That is better left to the Holy Spirit, as He intentionally leads each of His children into the same experiences and goals by separate paths, specifically tailored to develop intimacy with each one of us. My focus in this book is to simply help you identify the places He may be leading you to experience, and to encourage you not to stunt your own growth in bypassing those places and experiences which He so lovingly has designed for you.

---

[148] Refer to 2 Corinthians 5:18; paraphrased above.
[149] 2 Corinthians 5:18
[150] 2 Corinthians 5:20
[151] 1 Corinthians 12:31

Too many times the world—no, the world and the Church—will try to sell us forms and methods that relieve us of the very adversity God intends to use for our own tempering. In our pain and ignorance of the true love of God, we are all too often willing to buy such cheap goods.

Don't get me wrong; God does not afflict us and hurt us. He is not the author of pain and He does not bring death. However, in a world that is under the curse of death until Jesus returns, God will walk with us right through circumstances which accelerate the death of our "self." He joins us in the fire, in order that through trial we can see eternal glory manifest in our life. This is how we learn that God's glory actually comes as we are freed to live as sacrifices before Him and for others, knowing that God has already paid the price to raise us up.

> **God's glory actually comes as we are freed to live as sacrifices before Him and for others, knowing that God has already paid the price to raise us up.**

Before I close this chapter, I would like to point out some common attitudes which draw a disciple off the road of suffering and out of the position of brokenness:

Entitlement. If the God of our salvation saw fit to lower Himself on our behalf, how is it that we—no matter what price we think we have paid—deserve better than He did? Beware the spirit of entitlement which very easily rises up in the human heart. Religion has no more established method of destroying the heart than tricking us into believing that we have done enough to warrant a response from God. Entitlement is the archenemy of the grace of God and one of the quickest ways to poison the heart. When we believe we are entitled to anything more than what Christ went through, for any reason beyond His glory, we will begin to refuse to be broken and discard the need for humility.

Weariness. *The joy of the Lord is our strength*[152] is not just a children's church lyric. It is a statement of heaven's truth which prophesies all we need to live despite anything this life throws at us. The joy of the Lord is intimacy. Just as the joy of a lover is the actual experience of closeness to a person to which no other is entitled, so the joy of the Lord is the ability of His children to touch Him, taste Him, and simply be with Him in spite of any external trial.

When the actual satisfaction of intimacy and closeness with Him is lost, joy is lost as well. When joy is lost we immediately begin growing weary. Closeness and experience with Him bring the joy that refreshes the soul. When we lose that we grow tired and seek for ways to relieve the pain of our brokenness, rather than being willing to bear the brokenness so God can be exalted.

Frustration. Any expectation that is allowed to remain unexposed to the light and purified by contact with God's presence will eventually result in frustration and ultimately burnout. Many a man or woman of God can be heard talking about how they are experiencing burnout and are frustrated with life and ministry.

I have read many books and heard much teaching on good mental and physical exercises to avoid being overcome by frustration and maintain usefulness. But frustration cannot develop unless it is cultivated by striving for an outcome which is born in our own expectations or those we received from others.

Jesus said, "My yoke is easy and My burden is light."[153] When we find rest in trusting the Lord and doing only what He is doing when His grace is available to do it, there

---

[152] See Nehemiah 8:10.
[153] Matthew 11:30

is simply no room for frustration to grow. If we walk through discipleship as Holy Spirit leads, we will please God and find that only what God does can truly please us. In that place we do not grow uneasy, whether we are running hard or waiting long, because our only expectation is that He will always be with us and He will always do what is right and good. When we give no single expectation the room it requires to breed frustration in us, it will protect us from the urge to flee brokenness.

> **Ironically, greed might be the quickest setup for the kind of brokenness which a "broken disciple" is positioned to avoid.**

Greed. There is a way that we become convinced that all God has done in us is validation for us to pursue more of His blessing and power above compassion and love for others. Usually it is after some success, or under the influence of "successful" people, that we get hoodwinked into valuing ourselves selfishly and higher than we ought. It is too easy for the human soul to be so convinced of its own progress that we start to view ourselves as worth more by having more. In turn we begin to believe it is better for God and others that we move beyond the limitations of simplicity (another way of saying brokenness) in our life.

This mind-set values greater gifts and influence over the intentional development of vulnerable relationships. Accountability exits early in this process. Compromise, for the sake of power which we now believe we are "worthy" of wielding because we're "refined" enough to be independent, becomes a trademark of our morality. Ironically, greed might be the quickest setup for the kind of brokenness which a "broken disciple" is positioned to avoid. Jesus didn't mince words in telling His disciples about nailing the greedy human appetite to the cross. In Luke 14 and verse 33 (ESV), Jesus said, "So therefore, any one of you who does not renounce all that he has cannot be my disciple."

Be it greed, entitlement, or any diversion from the walk of a disciple, they all come coupled with two things: fear and doubt. The fear of man, fear of failure, or fear that God might not be everything the Gospel declares He is, sets us up to serve other gods and sacrifice at the altars named above. Doubt is the byproduct of surrendering to fear and creeps in when we subtly find ourselves looking to our own abilities rather than His. To be a disciple, as defined by Jesus, we must live by by the grace Jesus made available. He is eternal and only His eternal life flowing through us can produce lasting results in this temporary world.

Again in Luke 14, Jesus says that we must *forsake our own family, and even disregard our own life,* and that *whoever does not bear his own cross and pursue me cannot be my disciple.* We cannot do this by our own will or determination. Jesus's words even seem to contradict the human understanding of God's love. Brokenness prepares the human heart to submit regardless, which is the beginning of understanding God. Then, the contrast of experiencing His life through the brokenness tempers our instinct to rebel against Him because we know He is good even when circumstances and experiences aren't.

Only intentionally staying "poor in spirit" keeps us in the place we will see God. Remembering and remaining in our brokenness is how we stay alive in the glorious resurrection of Christ until He returns.

> But when that which is perfect has come,
> then that which is in part will be done away.
>
> —1 Corinthians 13:10

Part Three

The Acts

"What we do in partnership."

6

Abundant Life

ABUNDANT LIFE: AN INVITATION
by Michael Dow
Husband and Father
Cofounding Director, Burning Ones, Orlando, FL
One who rests in the abundance of Christ

REST:
  Relief or freedom, especially from anything that wearies, troubles, or disturbs.

ABUNDANT:
  Existing or available in large quantities; plentiful.

The gospel according to John, chapter 10:10 (NASB) quotes Jesus as saying, "I have come that they may have life, and have it abundantly." Abundant life is the condition God offers His children living in the midst of human chaos, in which the spiritual promise that everything available to Christ can be experienced in this life. Whether that translates to physical or material overflow at any given time, the man is not moved because the internal disposition flows out from Jesus Christ as the sole source, and therefore cannot ever be lacking. In my life, the doorway to this place is rest in Jesus Christ. For that reason, I want to invite all who read this to the rest that comes in knowing Jesus, and which produces in us the contentment and life which is, as Jesus described, "abundant."

Rest is something that has been made available to all men. In fact, the invitation into rest is something that is very possible for all to answer. Regardless of social status, background, or current financial standing, rest is waiting to be entered into by all who are willing to respond. Rest requires a response because rest is not initiated by man, but an invitation by God into a specific place. God has predetermined where rest can be found and fully enjoyed. God has set the terms for rest and invited men—even commanded them—that they enter in.[154]

> **Rest is not an outcome; rest is a Person, and His name is Jesus.**

You will never experience the beauty and fullness of abundant life, the life of internal richness despite any external circumstance, until you first relinquish your own self so that rest may be apprehended. Rest does not come by working your way into it. Rather, rest is found by responding to *Someone*. Rest is not an outcome; rest is a Person, and His name is Jesus.

In Matthew 11:28 (NASB) these words of Jesus echo out into the crowd, "Come unto Me, all of you who are weary and heavy-laden, and I will give you rest." Rest is only made possible by responding to this invitation. By coming to Jesus we find ourselves coming into rest, because true rest issues out of the life of Christ. Because Jesus Himself is life, and His life is at rest before the Father, He is able to offer us rest as He offers Himself.

---

[154] See Hebrews 3:7-4:13 for more on the "command" of rest.

Rest that has only had an effect on the appearance of our lives is not true rest. Rest that has only touched our tongues and the things we talk about but has not yet been able to settle the inner turmoil of life is not true rest. The truth of the matter is this: Rest cannot be faked; either it is real, and by being real, it is having a profound effect upon the entirety of our lives, or it has not yet been found.

Rest is not momentary or circumstantial. The wisdom of the world and the natural thought process of man lie to you and want you to believe that rest can only be occupied by those who have arrived at a special set of circumstances. This could not be further from the truth. Rest is eternal and immovable, because again, rest is a Person. Jesus rested in the storm because He knew that the storm answered to His Father, who above all else would never leave Him alone. This is the same rest we are called to before our heavenly Father, through a life lived in Christ.

> **Rest cannot be faked; either it is real, or it has not yet been found.**

I want to invite you into a wonderful place of complete rest that is beyond anything the world has to offer. I invite you into a place of rest that is set apart and untouched from the outcomes in your life. I invite you into an experience of rest that is constant, beautiful, and faithful. I invite you to respond to the invitation of Jesus today in your own heart and life.

Surrender all to Him, learn to trust in Him, and experience Him through trial and testing. There, in that place, you will learn of the Man who is both God and friend, brother and judge; the one you can trust with your past, present, and future. Then and only then will the abundance of rest birth within you the natural inflow of the life of Christ, which then effortlessly flows out to the world in abundance. Come to Him who is rest for your souls and live in His eternally abundant life, here and now.

* * *

CONTEXT

We have arrived at a turning point. Together, we have journeyed on the one bloody road of discipleship, having been confronted with the Gospel and submitted to its call. We have traversed the establishment of our identity and the redemption of creation through restored sonship in Christ. Having been broken as Peter, we have tasted of our own weakness and found life and freedom. In humility, Christ's redemption allows us to lavish the message of reconciliation on those whose thirsty souls need to drink of the Spirit's waters. Now we will venture together into abundant life. "It is no longer I who live," cried Paul, "but Christ who lives in me."[155]

> **Christ's redemption allows us to lavish the message of reconciliation on those whose thirsty souls need to drink of the Spirit's waters.**

As stated above in the invitation by Michael Dow, the term abundant life comes from John 10:10, where Jesus said, "The thief comes to steal, kill, and destroy, but I have come that they may have life, and life more abundant." Simply walking the road of a disciple, a true follower of Jesus Christ, will by the leading of the Spirit and the seasoning of experience bring you to a right understanding of the term, "abundant life." However, because of the most popular things being taught about this phrase

---

[155] See Galatians 2:20.

and the emphasis which is often misplaced, I want to help restore a right perspective. With the right understanding of the Father's heart we can have confidence in what Jesus said and align our own hearts rightly with His. ***All who believed were of one heart and one soul.***[156]

Once again, we are faced with undoing what marketability, numbers-driven ministry, and ministerial job security—not to mention blatant commercialization and profiteering of the Gospel—have perverted. You do not have to go far to hear someone use Christ's words in this verse as a foundation for teaching about financial prosperity.

In drawing people who seek material blessing over experiencing Christ Himself (which all of us must be wary of), this Scripture is regularly cut and pasted in a way that puts the emphasis on the word "abundant." Of course, the English/Western world's definition of abundance almost immediately leans toward material *things*. But the words as Christ Himself spoke them were not delivered in this way. Christ's emphasis was clearly on the word "life," not abundance.

Abundant was the adjective Jesus used to describe *life* in Him. The thief (in description of religious leaders who had put themselves between God and His children) comes to rob people of their inheritance in God, kill their spirits by enforcing false religious "authority," and destroy the kingdom Jesus is building. Christ came to put a stop to it by cutting out religious "middlemen" and directly providing people with a way into God's life.

Jesus was alluding to the words of Ezekiel, the Old Testament prophet, in order to liberate people's minds from the grip of religious leaders and their control. Let's look more closely at the Scripture for a moment, beginning in Ezekiel 34:2, and going through verse 17.

---

[156] Adapted from The Acts of the Apostles 4:32.

"Son of man, prophesy against the shepherds of Israel, prophesy and say to them, 'Thus says the Lord God to the shepherds: "Woe to the shepherds of Israel who feed themselves! Should not the shepherds feed the flocks?

You eat the fat and clothe yourselves with the wool; you slaughter the fatlings, but you do not feed the flock.

The weak you have not strengthened, nor have you healed those who were sick, nor bound up the broken, nor brought back what was driven away, nor sought what was lost; but with force and cruelty you have ruled them.

So they were scattered because there was no shepherd; and they became food for all the beasts of the field when they were scattered....

My flock was scattered over the whole face of the earth, and no one was seeking them or searching for them....

Behold, I am against the shepherds, and I will require My flock at their hand; I will cause them to cease feeding the sheep, and the shepherds will feed themselves no more; for I will deliver My flock from them; they will be food for their mouths no more....

I will feed My flock, and I will make them lie down....

Behold, I shall judge between sheep and sheep, between rams and goats."

When you see this text next to that of Jesus's words, it becomes very clear what Jesus meant. At the beginning of the John's tenth chapter, He describes His sheep as knowing God's voice, and in Jesus's care as their shepherd. We will pick it up in verse 7 for the sake of length. Let's take a look:

"Then Jesus said to them again, 'Most assuredly I say to you, I am the door of the sheep. All who ever came before me were thieves and robbers, but the sheep did not hear them. I am the door. If anyone enters by Me, he will be saved, and will go in and out and find pasture. The thief does not come except to steal, and to kill, and to destroy. *I have come that they may have life, and have it more abundantly.* I am the good shepherd. The good shepherd gives his life for the sheep. But a hireling, he who is not the shepherd, one who does not own the sheep, sees the wolf coming and leaves the sheep and flees; and the wolf catches the sheep and scatters them... he is a hireling and does not care about the sheep. I am the good shepherd...."

This is why it is so important to understand context in the Word of God. In no way whatsoever was Jesus promising wealth, or success, or anointing to people in the above verses. Most certainly, if you can claim those things as benefits of the *Abundant Life*, they were not His focus in this statement. *Abundant Life* was not spoken of by Jesus in reference to worldly success or gain. Beware of those who shift the focus of the Scripture to things that satisfy human lusts while disregarding the Lord's original intent. This is often a way for false shepherds seeking their own profit to play on human weakness.

> **Beware of those who shift the focus of the Scripture to things that satisfy human lusts while disregarding the Lord's original intent.**

When Jesus talked about "life more abundantly" He was referring to restoring the Good Shepherd to God's sheep. By Christ's definition, *Abundant Life* is that life in which God's flock know Him and His voice and live in freedom and fullness of access to the Kingdom in all of its safety and rest. Sure this may end up bearing physical or material benefits. But those were clearly not Christ's emphasis. Abundant life is life with Christ as our good shepherd where we, as sheep, are free to move between the pen and rich pasture.

THE BREATH OF LIFE

One of the first things I noticed in the days after my "Daddy" exchange with the Lord was a newfound ability to breathe deeply. Literally, in a physical sense, I felt refreshed and restored. My body received life and strength in a new intimacy with my Father. My mind was clear and my soul was at rest. For the first time in as long as I could remember, waking up was an exciting experience. It was as if I began to know what breathing in the life of God truly was.

The Genesis account of creation talks of God breathing life into the man as He formed him.[157] The Scripture describes the life of God being transferred to us by His breath, which is His Spirit; His life.[158] It is these types of moments with God by which some would define me as a mystic.[159] If the shoe fits, I will wear it. If I have learned one thing in my life, it is that God is real, and He really desires

---

[157] See Genesis 2:7.

[158] Later, Jesus would breathe on the disciples, saying, "Receive ye the Holy Spirit," indicating that the Spirit—the life—was the very breath of God; see John 20:22.

[159] Mysticism is the practice of self-contemplation and self-surrender as a means to unity with a deity. When Jesus is the center of such it is as John the Baptist said, *that we should decrease so He can increase.* Some fear the influence of Eastern religious traditions in Christian mysticism and rightfully guard against self-serving asceticism as a false form of piety. But to deny ourselves in order to make room for greater encounters with the person of God was a foundational approach even for Jesus. Some examples were when He fasted in the wilderness (see Matthew 4), withdrew and denied Himself sleep in prayer before being transfigured (see Luke 9), and when in isolated prayer He was so reduced that angels attended Him (see Luke 22). He also instructed His followers to fast for power and holiness (see Matthew 6; Matthew 17).

that I touch Him. He is a God of experience and demonstration. *Many signs and wonders were done among the people.*[160]

I can recall years of waking up with a boulder on my chest. There are literally years of my life which I can look back on in which stress, fear, and anxiety ruled my thinking. We know that these things alter our physical condition. It should be no mystery that spiritual connection and experience with the Lord do the same; and this before even factoring the supernatural transformational power that is in God.

Needless to say, having an encounter with God whereby I saw myself as closely attached to Him and felt immeasurably loved by Him in the midst of my own brokenness brought relief to the things which I couldn't bear. It truly changed everything. A new trust in God brought with it a new optimism. A new rest in my life brought with it a new steadiness. A new joy from the Lord carried a new courage.

Just as the day I repented and was relieved of the guilt of my sinful life, or the day I responded to His voice and was purged of my addictions, the day He met me in the intimacy of being a son washed me of the skepticism and cynicism that had lodged itself in my soul. Although the circumstances of my life were not suddenly altered in any noticeable way, I was instantly connected to the Source of all things.

I knew instinctively that I no longer needed to draw from the shallow pools of my own strength and resource. Neither did I have to look to any man, position, or influence other than my Daddy Himself. In one encounter, I was transformed from a man seeking the abundance in life into a child completely and recklessly lost in God's *Abundant Life*. Once again, my desire is simply to point

---

[160] Adapted from Acts 5:12.

you toward Him who was, Him who is, and Him who always will be. He is the very source of that life. ***Those who gladly received his word were baptized; and that day about three thousand souls were added.***[161]

HOW DEEP AND HOW WIDE

With the newfound ability to breathe came an awakening in certain areas of my life. As abundant life becomes our experience, it will have an expression. What has been formed in the quiet places between God and us begins to flow outward and manifest as actual change in our being and interactions with the world around us. Although the Lord will use incomplete people and their gifts to reach lost sheep, this is no substitute for those actually transformed, *being transformed*, into the likeness and image of Christ.

We have already mentioned those whose gifts seem to reap large rewards while their person falters in conveying God's love. That is an important dynamic to come to grips with in seeing the difference between living with abundance, yet not living Christ's abundant life. These are not one in the same, and what we are truly after as disciples is transformation into being one who is like the living Christ. That is the abundant life.

With that said, I want to talk about some of the ways in which abundant life has dynamically altered me. It has changed how I see, how I respond, and the attitudes of my heart in some very specific areas.

Obedience. Obedience is a subject on which our entire experience with the Lord hinges. If this book, or any other which talks about right relationship with God, doesn't lay out a clear position of obedience before the Lord and His voice, it is lacking. No matter which chapter

---

[161] Acts 2:41

I were to specifically highlight, the term obedience would make no difference. Whether we are at the point of decision with the Gospel, interacting with the Father in a personal way, being directed by the Spirit in a specific moment, or being guided through brokenness, obedience is the key to seeing His will revealed and the fullness of the Lord's intention unlocked.

Delay in obedience is a form of rebellion. Deferring on obedience will bring consequences into our life which are beyond the Lord's perfect will. Similarly, an attitude of ungratefulness in obeying smothers the release of many of the things the Lord intends to pour out on us as we obey. All of these are petulant ways we wave our fists in protest even as we might actually do the thing the Lord wants. It should be obvious that these attitudes taint our actions. For this reason, I have chosen to bring obedience to light in the shadow of abundant life.

> **Abundant life is a forward position, an offensive position of the heart that has learned to delight in the Lord through trial and pain.**

Abundant life is, in itself, a fundamental recalibration of the heart and attitude before the Lord. Abundant life is a forward position, an offensive position of the heart that has learned to delight in the Lord through trial and pain, and now approaches the Lord in every way—from fulfilling promises to submitting to His discipline—with enthusiasm and joy.

Hopefully you can see why abundant life is an integral part of the discussion of obedience to the Lord. When we can turn our view of the word obedience from a labor that implies some loss or pain, and *turn into* obedience as a place of complete life which bears freedom every time we rightfully obey, life will change. In the abundant life obedience becomes a natural expression that doesn't need to hem and haw over when and how to follow instruction, but instead jumps "all in" knowing that any leap into the things God is doing is a leap into living waters. ***Peter and the other apostles replied, "We must obey God…."***[162]

Rest. I am a coffee nut. I drink it strong, black, and sweet; multiple times each day. I go to bed late and rise early. I have four children, travel for a living, and very often spend long hours working in strange environments where the language, culture, and the way of thinking are foreign. I push my body, test my mind, and often do this with the lives of others in my care. I am always tired. But I do not grow weary. I do not live battling burnout.

With a clear conscience I can say that rest has become the bulwark of my approach to life. I purpose to make decisions from this place alone. My wife and I wage war against anything, any thought and any relationship, that seeks to pull us away from being at rest. This is because once you have experienced trusting in the Lord with all of your heart and the constancy that is the Father of Lights,[163] you realize that rest is not laziness or the lack of doing. Rest, like brokenness, is a part of who we become in Jesus.

As Michael Dow shared in this chapter's opening, Hebrews says as God's children we are commanded to enter rest. Hebrews posits rest as a prerequisite of faith.[164] That's because rest in the Lord is trust which invades and permeates all of our being. Many try to substitute a form of Sabbath ritual for true rest. Many confuse doing nothing,

---

[162] Acts 5:29 (NIV)

[163] Refer to James 1:17,18 for the beautiful description of God as the Father of Lights.

[164] Read Hebrews from start to finish. You will see the narrative arc goes from rest (and the lack thereof) before God, and what the results are—either being cut off from Him or walking in radical faith.

or recreation, with rest. Although these can be done in rest, none of them are truly restful apart from real peace in Christ.

Think about this: if Genesis says that the Lord rested from the work of creation on the seventh day, then when exactly was it that He went back to work? Is it possible the rest we are called into isn't the rest of *doing nothing*, that maybe we have lost some of the spiritual life which allows us to both be fully at rest while being alive and active in Him? Is it possible that like a woman carrying a baby, that the moment of the Lord's rest from creation—like the moment of labor for the mother—was simply a move from the work that has no current satisfaction to a new reality which shares in the reward of actually having the baby? If anything the work increases, but now the child is there being raised to join in the mother's present and future work. The child is both the work *and* the reward.

> **Rest is the fundamental disposition of one who has come to know abundant life.**

The Lord once said to me that, "NOTHING…is impossible with God."[165] Did you get it? Nothing, as in nothing happening, nothing moving, or nothing being accomplished, is impossible with God. With Him *something* is always happening. Rest is the fundamental disposition of one who has come to know abundant life. Abundant life is established on a position of victorious rest no matter what the situation looks like around us. ***He threw them into the inner prison…. But Paul and Silas were praying and singing hymns of praise to God.***[166]

---

[165] Refer to Luke 1:37, "For with God, nothing is impossible."
[166] Adapted from Acts 16:24,25 (NIV).

A new family. Before being broken, arrogance and fear were masters of most of my relationships. Even when I could act the part, I can honestly say that the internal man didn't feel very Christian, especially in relation to *other Christians*. I was truly the older brother in the story of the prodigal son.[167] I became a man of criticism and comparison. But the abundant life of Christ has filled me with a love for others which was not of my own design.

Although I wanted to love people for the sake of God's approval, I really would have preferred to be able to criticize and compare myself out of relationships with those who didn't meet my standards. But breathing in the life of the Spirit and walking in His freedom—the hallmarks of the *Abundant Life*—energized me to extend the same to others. The compassion and love for others in need that was birthed in my brokenness now had the passion to relentlessly give away the same Christ I was experiencing. Almost instantly Jesus's life flowing through me gave a certain value to people I previously discredited. The Body of Christ was now *my* family. **Continuing daily with one accord in the temple, and... from house to house, they ate their food with gladness and simplicity of heart.**[168]

Giving. How can I explain the difference between generosity and duty? This is like trying to explain motivation in terms of love, rather than fear or ambition. To someone who has never been loved; it makes no sense. It sounds great, seems right, and would probably work in a perfect world, but this world isn't perfect, right? *Not so fast.*

To the person found and undone by love, it is the only way. No, this world isn't perfect, but we are—and are being—perfected in Christ. So from the inflow of God's generous love, which characterizes the relationship that

---

[167] See Luke 15:11-32 for the story of the "prodigal son."
[168] Acts 2:46

abundant life is built on, flows out the desire to see what you have and what you wish for lavished on others even more than yourself.

How do you become a person who actually believes and experiences that it is greater to give than to receive? By walking the bloody road of discipleship straight into the abundance of Christ. Christ gives more of Himself to those who seek to be poured out. Once you can step past the five bucks in your pocket, and tap into the vastness of God's heart that is flowing through you, it's not so hard to get over the fact that all you can "sow" may be pennies. Giving is about the resources God has, and not those you lack. *This is not an offering message.* I don't care if you are a visibly generous millionaire or if you never give a dollar again. One who walks in the *Abundant Life* is not his own, and therefore is not called to give percentages. We are called to *completely* give of ourselves, *all* of the time.

> **All that you have, all that you are, and all that you will be is the sum of Christ in you.**

All that you have, all that you are, and all that you will be is the sum of Christ in you. Your person, your time, your relationships, your money, and everything else that can follow the word "your" actually aren't yours at all. Living the abundant life brings this reality into being an uncompromising part of how we live. **Nor was there anyone among them who lacked.**[169]

Living in second. I hear the shouts of resistance, "I am the head and not the tail in Christ!" I know the reaction of many of hearing that we "learn to live in second" goes against every ambitious, self-fulfilling American desire to

---

[169] Adapted from Acts 4:34-35.

have "authority in Christ." But we have already beaten this to its bloody crucifixion.

Substitute this with the entire premise of brokenness. Change "living in second" with the paradigm of giving, which we just discussed. Abundant life is a life of love. Love does not seek its own.[170] Love seeks for another before itself; ALWAYS. There is nothing more to say.

When I began to live in the abundant life given to me by Christ, for the first time I was truly learning the joy of standing in support of others, even at the expense of my own dreams. I continue to be taken to places and given opportunities by which I can lift others as they receive the things I desire. The abundant, overflowing, never-ending life which Christ lives through me has a constant supply. I cannot run the tap dry. We need to be careful not to live this way for seasons until we (or others) decide we have paid enough. The well of humility can always go deeper.

No matter how many times I sacrifice in order to lift someone else, there is always another opportunity coming for me to put off my own accomplishments for somebody else's success. I have heard Evangelist Bonnke say that "honor is the currency of heaven." In my bloody walk of discipleship, he has repeatedly been proved right.

If God truly is our source and supply, then He can never be exhausted and there will never be a limit to what He is able to do, even when we spend ourselves lifting others and disregarding our own advancement. In fact, it pleases the Father's heart to have kids who give their lives for their family.

Prayer and faith. Pastor Bill Johnson teaches that we should encourage people to pray every time like it is their first. It is his way of saying we should stand boldly before

---

[170] See 1 Corinthians 13 for the definition of love.

the throne of grace, as Paul wrote.[171] Abundant life settles the fear of not having prayers answered with the knowledge that eternity is established within us.

When my son was just six weeks old, he spiked a fever that we couldn't immediately control. Because of his young age, the doctors told us to get him to the hospital for fear he might have an infection that his young immune system couldn't fight.

My wife went to the ER and I was a little late to arrive coming from work. By the time I got there, they were transporting him by ambulance to the regional children's hospital and requesting permission to do a spinal tap. We were a little freaked out to say the least. I drove behind the ambulance, needing to bring a vehicle to the new hospital.

As I began to pray for my son, fear overshadowed me and I wept and pled with the Lord, unable to stand in any surety of the outcome. Almost immediately, I felt the presence of God sweep over me, calming me. Then I felt Him ask me a question, "Why are you praying something you don't even believe?" Those words broke me. He was right again, and I was humbled by God, again. He kept speaking, "What are you afraid of? I am with you." I could feel my spirit rising. Again, the Voice came to my heart, "Pray like you know Me and like I know you. I love your son more than you. Don't pray in fear that I won't answer…like you might be disappointed."

I began to be filled with a joy that certainly didn't match the moment, and it was as if I heard Him say, "Don't ever

---

[171] Hebrews 4:16

pray like that again." Then out it came. I prayed for my son, not with the assurance that I knew the answer, but with absolute assurance that the God who loved us both, *was* the answer. *Abundant Life* is reflected in the way we pray and stand in faith. **They were all filled with the Holy Spirit, and they spoke the Word of God with boldness.**[172]

Discovery. There was a time in the weeks after we returned from Africa in our second year on the mission field where I was floundering a bit. I had heard some things in my spirit which I was believing for in faith, but for several reasons which I see now, things just weren't coming to pass at that time. The single greatest reason was that the things I heard, although they were the Word of God and aligned with biblical truth, weren't developed enough within me to bear fruit yet. I wasn't mature enough to collect on some of the deposits in my heart. Certain things, if we were to receive them a day early, would actually ruin us.

> **Certain things, if we were to receive them a day early, would actually ruin us.**

One particular day I was wrestling in prayer, asking God to show me what was wrong. I remember listening to Jason Upton sing Psalm 23 as I sat in stillness on the couch. *Surely goodness and mercy cover me. All the days of my life they cover me....* Then, I saw in my heart a picture of myself putting a cassette into a player. It was as if the Lord said to me, "John, you know exactly what to put in and you know exactly what you expect to come out. You measure out the right amount of study, the perfect dose of prayer, and deliver it in the right words, thinking you will

---

[172] Acts 4:31

produce what you want in any given moment. What if My mercies really are new every morning?"[173]

He then asked, "Why have you stopped coming like a child, with the wonder and awe that every time you come to Me might be totally new and totally different than the last?" Remember what we are talking about here? *Abundant Life* isn't measured on earthly scales. When Jesus spoke the words in John 10, He was referring to the endless measures of heaven which are found in God. We are called to a life of discovery in Christ, not a life of learning how to do what the last guy did or memorizing a formula that can produce some sort of relatively effective response. After all, *this is God* we are talking about. God is alive. God is endless, and He wants to be discovered. **God worked unusual miracles.**[174]

PARADOX

I hope by now a singular theme is emerging for you. For me it is clear that there is, and never will be, any other theme than Jesus Christ. Jesus Christ is the evidence of God in word and deed, manifest in the flesh. He is the door, the gate, *the Way, the Truth, and the Life.* The Gospel hinges on Him, because it *is* Him.

Sonship is the story of Jesus and His Father opening the door for us to the same relationship. Brokenness is the place where sonship meets the pavement, or if not, where our egos one day will. Walking through these places ushers us into the abundant life of Christ. We are merging ourselves into the way of the Kingdom. We need to get the revelation that all of these places both intersect and run parallel at the same time.

---

[173] See Lamentations 3:22,23.
[174] Acts 19:11

An undeniable paradox exists simply in the union between God and mankind. What *we are not* is being drawn into what *He is*. And although there is a certain "progress" that should happen in our lives, we also have all of God the moment we respond to the Gospel. We are fully sons, fully broken, and fully brought into abundant life. This is all happening at once, and as it does, we progressively learn to experience and express Christ more than before.

Don't ask me to scientifically or even theologically dissect this paradox. That is definitely for another time, and most likely for another author. But the dynamic is true because we are nothing and He is everything. Because He is everything we have also become spiritually the same. Do you see where I am going with this? Any insufficiency we experience is temporary. In Him, the fixed position is now abundant life. It is only a matter of living in this reality despite the false testimony of the dying world around you.

As Christ makes us alive, we are free to dream again in the innocence of a child.

There is nothing strange about going through some of the same lessons. There is nothing weird when one area of our life seems to be firing on all cylinders, yet others can feel like they are coming apart at the seams. That's because for a disciple what is and always should seem constant, is Christ. Our growth and progress is important. Stagnation in our walk with the Lord is really a form of regression. But our performance is not the measure of the Lord in our life. It is *a* measure. It is *an* expression. The presence of Jesus's person and the allegiance of a man to the Lord's heart will be the greatest measure of abundant life flowing through that person.

Only the Lord sees the full picture and He dictates the life we lead and its "fruitfulness." As Christ makes us alive, we are free to dream again in the innocence of a child. We can make mistakes without fear of being destroyed for it. When Christ lives in us, our creativity is released and we aren't bound by pain or lust in what we express. When Jesus Christ is alive in us, we aren't stripped of our identity because God isn't seeking to pasteurize the richness out of His children.

God, in His mercy, simply uses breaking as a way of taking us to where we have nothing to lose in how we live life before Him. In Him, we always have everything to gain and abundant life to give; we can live wide open, pedal to the metal, and totally abandoned to His love and what it produces through us. *I do not count my life dear to myself, so that I may finish my race with joy.*[175]

It is the relationship with Him that drives the bus. It is because that relationship has been established as real and alive—not just some mental or spiritual exercise—that the enemy has been disarmed from taking my failures or shortcomings and turning them into total losses. I am telling you that we no longer need to live in fear of judgment, but only encouraged by the goodness of God in any temporary condition, so long as we know Him and are known by Him.

Scripture tells us that love covers a multitude of sins. Love is not a feeling. Love is an action. It is an attitude and a shared exchange between the Lord and us. If we are consummated into that love, consecrated and set apart by that love, and if we remain connected through love to the Father's heart, then we can be steady in all of our ways. His ways overtake us. Rather than grappling with sin, we will grieve at the thought of grieving Him and not settle in trying to balance what is permissible in our relationship with Him.

---

[175] Acts 20:24

Abundant life is not flashy. It is not man-pleasing or self-glorifying. It is not focused on this world or any of its wares. But abundant life is just that—abundant—and it is accessible, even necessary, to live out the destiny to which God has called His children. Now, breathe! ***There came a mighty sound from heaven, as of a rushing mighty wind, and it filled the house where they were sitting.***[176]

> But in all things we commend ourselves as ministers of God: in patience, in tribulations…as sorrowful, yet always rejoicing; as poor, yet making many rich; as having nothing, and yet possessing all things.
>
> —2 Corinthians 6:4,10

---

[176] Acts 2:2

7

Living Stones

LIVING STONES: AN INVITATION
by Lenny Maglione
Husband and Father
Cofounding Pastor, Church of the Harvest, Riverhead, NY
A living stone

Consider these facts outlining the condition of your generation, taken from a *TIME* magazine article by Joel Stein on May 20, 2013:

> "The incidence of narcissistic personality disorder is nearly three times as high for people in their 20s as for the generation that's now 65 or older…58% more college students scored higher on a narcissism scale in 2009 than in 1982. Millennials got so many participation trophies growing up…40% believe they should be promoted every two years, regardless of performance. They are fame-obsessed: three times as many middle school girls want to grow up to be a personal assistant to a famous person as want to be a Senator…They're so convinced of their own greatness that [studies reveal] the guiding morality of 60% of millennials in any situation is that they'll just be able to feel what's right. Their development is stunted: more people ages 18 to 29 live with their parents than with a spouse…And they are lazy. In 1992…80% of people under 23 wanted to one

day have a job with greater responsibility; 10 years later, only 60% did."

Indeed, this is a sobering commentary on the continuing decline of our culture. Contrast this to the Spirit of God that is drawing you to imitate the heart of Christ with these words to the Father, "Not my will, but thine."[177]

John the Baptist said it this way, "He must increase and I must decrease."[178] The "I must decrease" is significant. There is no journey into discipleship without the call to lose yourself in Christ, for God's own sake. The apostle Peter implies the same in 1 Peter 2:4-5 (NIV), "As you come to Him, *the* Living Stone…you also, like living stones, are being built into a spiritual house to be a holy priesthood, offering spiritual sacrifices acceptable to God through Jesus Christ." You, "like a *living* stone" are honed out of the quarry of humanity and fitted into the temple of the living God. In your generation it seems the quarries are depleted of usable stone.

Wait, God is calling me, to be a *what*…? That's right, a living stone after Jesus. In Ephesians 2:20-22 (NIV), the apostle Paul, speaking of the New Testament Church, goes further by saying that we are "built on the foundation of the apostles and prophets, with Christ Jesus himself as the *chief cornerstone.*…" Paul continues, "In him the whole building is joined together and rises to become a holy temple in the Lord…in him you too are being built together to become a dwelling in which God lives by his Spirit."

As you turn to Jesus, He draws you into and upon Himself, the chief cornerstone of all living stones; who is alive, eternal, and unchanging. To come is to throw yourself on Him, allowing Him to break you of your self-will.

---

[177] Luke 22:42 (KJV)
[178] John 3:30

In Luke 20:18 (NASB) Jesus said, "Everyone who falls on that stone will be broken to pieces; but on whomever it falls, it will scatter him like dust."

But you are not condemned to being scattered like dust. Instead when you fall on Him you are then reformed, refined, and fitted as a living stone into the House of God. The physical temple no longer remains, but a spiritual temple is being erected that is accessible to all people, anyplace in the world. Now a spiritual temple stands and continues to expand with each added stone where God's presence dwells.

> **It's fairly obvious that you cannot extract raw stones from the ground and easily fit them into the design for a temple.**

God's people are His dwelling place, the place where He *now* lives by His Spirit; accessible to a lost and dying world, anywhere on the planet, *right now*. How awesome is this calling?

Christ Himself has invited you to be a part of the dwelling which displays God's presence in the earth. You are actually chosen as the building material. But beware; there is a cost. It will take nothing less than total surrender. In the same way Christ surrendered to God and His disciples to the Christ, so are we called.

It's fairly obvious that you cannot extract raw stones from the ground and easily fit them into the design for a temple. They must each be fashioned and shaped before being placed according to the architect's scheme. Consequently, some very unique-looking stones may not look so distinctive after being refined and molded for fitting. You must allow the hammer and chisel of God to do their perfect work on your raw disposition and character in order to produce a finely made stone, acceptable to Him in both style and function, for placement in the building. *He must increase, and I must decrease.*

There is more to these living stones, you see. "Living stones" differ from normal bricks or rocks in that living stones are not only built into the temple, but they are also active in the temple as the holy priesthood. Each living stone is positioned to offer sacrifices. These sacrifices are no longer those of animals, but spiritual sacrifices which each of us offer for the salvation and sanctification of others.

The apostle Paul writes in his epistle to the Romans, "I urge you, brethren, by the mercies of God, to present your bodies a living and holy sacrifice, acceptable to God, which is your spiritual service of worship."[179] We read in the epistle to the Hebrews, "Through Him then, let us continually offer up a sacrifice of praise to God…the fruit of lips that give thanks to His name." Continuing, the author pens, "And do not neglect doing good and sharing, for with such sacrifices God is pleased."[180] As you say yes, your very existence becomes a continual offering of your prayers, praise, and deeds, to God. The living stones, now following the example of Jesus Christ, offer themselves on behalf of others. The priest represents man to God and God to man. Yes, his chief duty is sacrifice; nevertheless, he also is an intercessor and mediator who brings the message of God to humanity and represents people before God.

The living stones, now following the example of Jesus Christ, offer themselves on behalf of others.

So, in light of a declining culture and the glorious temple Christ is building, you are invited to finish the race.

---

[179] Romans 12:1 (BSB)
[180] Hebrews 13:5,6 (NASB)

Complete the course![181] Allow Christ to shape and place you into the House of God, which is a beacon to the world, with your life as a continual offering for others. Many come to Him who will not work to this end. But disciples do not just depend on Christ as some form of "fire" insurance against the penalty of selfishness or to satisfy the conscience while still belonging to the world. A disciple must be fashioned into a living stone, built on Christ, and added to that spiritual house in which God lives, walks, and works to reveal Himself.

* * *

A CALL TO COMMUNION

Before I press on, I'd like to visit the setting inside the spiritual temple of God of which my dear friend, Lenny Maglione, spoke of above. Remember, this "temple" is the building which is made of living stones—disciples—who are bound together, serving each other in love and dedication, serving the Lord in worship, and serving those outside the temple with sacrifice and forgiveness.

> **Remember that the temple does not exist if we remove the people.**

Remember that the temple does not exist if we remove the people. It is a spiritual dwelling place of God's presence which rests in and among His children in their fellowship and life together. With Jesus as its High Priest, the Church isn't a physical building or a place in your town. The Church is us—it's you, and it's me, and all of those who

---

[181] Paul uses these terms in 1 Corinthians 9:23-25 and 2 Timothy 4:7, referring to enduring to the end in a victorious walk with Christ.

share identity in Christ. Without us, there is no spiritual temple to speak of. Why do I belabor this point? Because I want to peer inside this "building" for a moment and speak of what happens within its walls.

Go with me once again to John's gospel, chapter 13. I want to look back at the scene John describes just before the place we picked it up back in the chapter on brokenness. Verse 3 is where I would like to begin.

> "Jesus, knowing that the Father had given all things into His hands, and that He had come from God and was going to God, rose from supper and laid aside His garments, took a towel and girded Himself. After that, He poured water into a basin and began to wash the disciples' feet, and to wipe them with the towel with which He was girded.
>
> Then He came to Simon Peter, and Peter said to Him, 'Lord, are You washing my feet?' Jesus answered and said to him, 'What I am doing you do not understand now, but you will know after this.'"

It is important to get a grip on what was going on here. These guys have lived with each other for three years now. They have followed the man they believe to be the Messiah, and the One God has continuously validated with all incredible revelation, with signs and with wonders like they have never seen before. And He was about to wash their feet.

It is important to understand Middle Eastern culture a little in order to grasp the gravity of Jesus's actions. Status, age, and a series of other traditional factors create a culture of respect and honor which people do not violate. In our Western thinking, we weigh disrespect, or what we view as the simple crossing of these barriers, based on the urgency of the moment. Be it financial accounting, safety, general common sense—or whatever else—if the reasons outweigh the value of the respect or authority in the relationship, we generally cross that line with ease.

Not in Eastern cultures. In the Eastern, or Middle Eastern world for that matter, people live and die on the honor due a person based on a specific covenant made or historical and cultural boundaries that trump our Western logic. With that said, their Master, Teacher, and MESSIAH KING is about to stoop to the level of servanthood, and with a towel, bow before them and wash their feet. Not only is this an immense honor to them, but it is also such a gesture that even the thought of it indicts them because they have not first offered such to Jesus.

Keep in mind that Jesus is doing this with the foreknowledge of the Spirit, which the disciples are not privy to. Even though He tells them this will be their last time together, they don't get it, and their ignorance to what Jesus is about to suffer on their behalf doesn't stop the Savior from spilling humility and love on them.

Not only is He sharing Himself in the deepest way, during the hour of His hardest testing, but the disciples don't have a clue what's at stake. The way He does it smashes every norm as to what should happen in this moment and only amplifies the severity of His actions. In their world, had they understood, they should be bestowing on Jesus every bit of praise and honor they had. But Jesus bends to them, leading heaven in the same nod of selfless love to this filthy world.

With this in mind, we can understand Peter's protest and get a feel for the scene John wrote out for us. In verse 8 we see Peter's demonstrative and compensatory chivalry declaring,

"'You shall never wash my feet!'

Jesus answered him, 'If I do not wash you, you have no part with Me.'

Simon Peter said to Him, 'Lord, not my feet only, but also my hands and my head!'

Jesus said to him, 'He who is bathed needs only to wash his feet, but is completely clean; and you are clean....'"

Again, let's take inventory. At this juncture, Peter realizes his need before the Lord. Having subjected himself to the Gospel daily but not yet living by the Spirit and immersed in the abundant life of a son who has passed through brokenness, Peter feels compelled to get "saved all over again." Jesus gently explains that grace has already done its work; that having been in relationship with Jesus has made him clean. He then alludes that since Peter has been with Him (*abiding* in His presence[182]) he has been cleansed (saved) already; that all Peter really needs now is to have his feet washed in an act of intimate honor and love. Our feet represent the lowest part of us, which is bound by the laws of physics to stay in contact with the (sinful) world. For Peter, this washing came as part of the most sacred meal of the Jewish year, Passover.

What I am trying to show you is that in this moment Jesus establishes that He knows there are still some things that attach themselves to those who walk with Him. He is saying that even though Peter doesn't fully comprehend or live in a complete understanding of what Christ has done or *is doing*, He honors Peter for his *abiding* with the Lord. While doing this, Jesus is instituting a powerful family tradition that He wants to continue in the "spiritual house" made of living stones, which will stand and grow after He leaves the earth.

---

[182] See John 15 for more on "abiding in Christ."

T. Austin Sparks writes in his book *Spiritual Senses*, "Independent action is as dangerous as dislocation—it robs of covering and protection and exposes to enemy forces."[183] God's people are not only the implements of washing and restoration, but also the very shields and weapons of warfare; the very brick and mortar in the building of His Kingdom on the earth. It's important to know that when we are separate from Him or our spiritual brethren, we are responsible for our own losses. We have no one to wash our feet.

Read a little more with me into the Scripture, picking up in verse 14: "If I then, your Lord and Teacher, have washed your feet, you also ought to wash one another's feet. For I have given you an example, that you should do as I have done to you…" Of course, we know from Matthew's chapter 26 account of the Gospel that the meal they ate together before this washing was the meal by which Jesus also compelled them to continue together sharing the breaking and receiving of bread and the lifting and drinking of the cup in remembrance of Him.

Why is this significant? How does this relate to Peter and Paul's call to be *Living Stones*, the holy priesthood, set before the world as the dwelling place of God's presence? If the spiritual building which we corporately represent is the "dwelling place" of the Father, and we are His kids, and He wants more kids to make a bigger house, all resulting in more of His glory invading the darkness of the earth, then I ask you to consider the picture Jesus paints of what God's family looks like within His house!

Jesus's final prayer, found in John 17, is a plea to the Father that the original disciples would know Him so intimately that it would bring them into a fellowship—a

---

[183] T. Austin Sparks, *Spiritual Senses* (Life Sentence Publishing), Kindle edition.

communion[184]—with the Father and the Holy Spirit which is so deep that it would draw them together in love for each other and radically display God's glory.

In the changing of water to wine at Cana,[185] Jesus first revealed a glimpse of who He was, and of God's glory come to the world. In the breaking of bread, He fed thousands.[186] Again in this moment, with the sharing of a meal—bread and wine—as a family does on the eve of a great holiday, Jesus again reveals who He was. Over a meal He tells His followers to always remember the moment and honor Him by continuing it, and then begins to wash them with the same instructions: *Do this for each other when I am gone.*

> **Jesus's great parting words are a call to do, and be, as a family is and does.**

Do you see it? Jesus's great parting words; His manifesto—the closing salvo by which He declares, instructs, and compels the disciples and those who will follow them—are a call to do, and be, as a family is and does.[187] *As the family of God!* The family of God brings life and glory to the world. The family of God shares the most intimate places and intimate moments together. The family of God doesn't criticize, divide, and compare; we are to bow before each other, disrobed and unarmed, in order that we might wash and restore each other. Not once, but mile after mile, year after year, until that day when the Lord comes again

---

[184] Suggested reading on the topic of communion: *Jesus the Bridegroom* by Brant Pitre.
[185] See John 2.
[186] See Matthew 14:19; 15:36; Mark 6:41.
[187] Suggested reading on the topic of "the family of God" and familial "fellowship," read *True Fellowship* by Art Katz.

and finally sets all things in order. *"That they may receive forgiveness of sins and a place among those who are sanctified by faith in me."*[188]

* * *

"But Lord, You cannot leave us! What will we do? Who will we be? *How will they know us?"* James pleaded.

Jesus replied, but not as they expected, "A new commandment I give to you, that you love one another; as I have loved you, you shall love each other." There was no commissioning of power, no talk of healing or of the casting out of demons. But with the authority of heaven and the wisdom of the ages on His lips, Jesus planted them as bearers of the Kingdom come, saying, "By this all will know that you are My disciples, if you have love—the Father's love, for which I have paid with My blood—if you have this love, one for another."[189]

This, my friend, is the *glory* housed within the temple, not built with human hands, but built by Christ, on Him who is the chief cornerstone, and with you and me as its *living stones.* This is the greatest work of the evangelist; this is the deepest word which the prophet can deliver. The love of Christ which *remembers* Him, *joins* us in Him, and *invites* them through Him, is the reason we walk the same bloody road which Christ Himself paved—the glorious road of discipleship.

THIS ROAD LEADS TO SOMEWHERE

While earlier we established that the road of discipleship never ends, we have also discussed the paradox of that road,

---

[188] Acts 26:18 (ESV)
[189] Adapted from the account in John's gospel, chapter 13.

whereby in having no end, each step is a destination. In every part of the process, Jesus is being glorified through what is happening to us and through us. In his book titled, *And They Crucified Him*, Art Katz writes, in description of how Jesus's very act of death brought salvation to the Roman soldier:

> "Though the centurion had seen numbers of men squirming, groaning, and cursing while being crucified, there was something about the manner of Jesus' dying that drew him to recognize His true identity. Though Jesus had performed many miracles, it was this decisive testimony of Himself—that is, the very manner of his dying—that brought what may well have constituted salvation for a man who otherwise would have eternally perished as a sinner."[190]

This helps to explain part of how we, as priests, are also the sacrifice that makes room for the atonement and salvation of others. It's not that we are worthy to be their savior, but as ambassadors for *The Savior* we act in representation of Him. We live displaying His finished work in an ongoing example of selfless love. Then, in being the sacrifice we lay ourselves down in order to draw others to Jesus and extend forgiveness to them; we are resurrected in Christ and as sons of the King, given a special authority upon the earth. **"Open their eyes, so that they may turn from darkness to light and from the power of Satan to God."**[191]

As kings, we enforce our Father's Kingdom. In this identity we stand in the assurance that signs and wonders follow the preaching of the Gospel.[192] It is how we overcome the enemy, as John the Revelator wrote, "by the *word*

---

[190] Art Katz, *And They Crucified Him* (Bemidji, MN: Burning Bush Press, 2011), Kindle edition.
[191] Acts 26:18 (ESV)
[192] See Mark 16:15-20.

of their testimony and the blood of the Lamb."[193] Our testimony means that we are a real part of this. Our history with Christ influences our world.

The road we are on has been marked out and made clear for us by the blood of Jesus. The one bloody road of discipleship leads us on a journey of building a testimony which, being coupled with the blood of Christ, fleshes out the defeat of Satan. Our life in Christ is the ultimate proof of the demise of sin and death. Inasmuch as we are laid down and surrendered to Christ living through us, we are also recreated as individual children, with individual gifts, and fitting into the Body of Christ uniquely. The Holy Spirit literally co-authors a testimony with us through the power endued us by *the blood of the Lamb.* As we press on toward a conclusion together, the "Living Stones" illustration both Peter and Paul left for us serves to encapsulate this paradox of simultaneous living and dying quite possibly better than any other discussion point in all of the Bible.

> **Our life in Christ is the ultimate proof of the demise of sin and death.**

NOT JUST ANOTHER BRICK IN THE WALL

Pink Floyd, the uber-famous psychedelic rock band, sang a song titled, "Another Brick in the Wall," which distilled one of the greatest fears of humanity. The lyrics breathe out rebellion against the writer's school days, in which he experienced the loss of his identity through the abuse and institutionalization programmed into his entire generation. Gaining in a driving, yet haunted, chant-like chorus, the song culminates in this:

---

[193] Revelation 12:11

I don't need no arms around me
And I don't need no drugs to calm me.
I have seen the writing on the wall.
Don't think I need anything at all.
No! Don't think I'll need anything at all.
All in all it was all just bricks in the wall.
All in all you were all just bricks in the wall.[194]

I can remember singing these words out while feeling disenfranchised, wounded, and fearing that life was a series of ambushes. I lived as a "taker", and I feared that those positioned to care for and nurture me were only using me for their own benefit. Spurred on by the relentless human tendency, I drove toward independence. *I didn't think I needed anything at all.* I would never be just a brick in anyone's wall; not a family's, not a corporation's, not a nation's, and especially not the Church's. Institutionalization and *domestication* were quite possibly the worst destinies I could imagine. How ironic it is that my entire life, everything I am working toward and everything I am surrendered to, is pointing toward this one thing: that I would be *just another living stone* in my Father's building.

Jesus Christ, in His first coming, was not the ultimate expression of God to the world. He was the complete expression. He was the true expression. Even now, in the way He relates and interacts with us, He is the perfect expression. However, God has designed the redemption process, with Jesus one day coming again to finalize His marriage to the Church—*His bride*—to include the glorification of that bride in the blossoming of a process of corporate discipleship. Jesus, made manifest to the world through the power of the Holy Spirit, awaits the Father's

---

[194] Pink Floyd, "Another Brick In the Wall Lyrics," *Pink-Floyd-Lyrics.com*, http://www.pink-floyd-lyrics.com/html/another-brick-in-the-wall-lyrics.html.

final establishment of a people who will be spiritually presented to Jesus as a bride.[195] The Bride of Christ corporately houses and reveals God's agape love just as Jesus did. This is the *ultimate* expression God has chosen: Jesus the Firstborn, clothed in the Father's glory, and partnered with us as His eternal Bride.

What is being played out, through Him shaping individual living stones, fusing them together by His Spirit, and empowering them to envelope the earth in His glory, is something like a dress rehearsal for eternity. We will one day be united to Him as glorified spirit beings, and in this age He uses our own brokenness as a sharpening stone of sorts—a grinding stone that we willingly submit ourselves to—in order to be refined into the image of His Son. In this way our transition to His holiness is the natural progression of the grace over our lives.

> **This is the ultimate expression God has chosen: Jesus the Firstborn, clothed in the Father's glory, and partnered with us as His eternal Bride.**

As much as Jesus was completely man and completely submitted to His Father while in this world, He was also supernaturally born to the world by the Spirit. He carried no baggage. He simply took off His godliness to assume our humanity.[196] Yes, this was a glorious act, but how much more glorious is it that there could be a people in the earth who walk as He did, love each other as He loved us, and who discover, through the walk of a disciple and the placement in His spiritual building, abundant life above anything this world has to offer!

---

[195] See Revelation 19:5-9.
[196] See Philippians 2:7.

It is an absolutely necessary part of God's eternal plan that we savor all of the personal and individual interactions and revelations that occur in a relationship with the Father. But these individual steps take us into our place as living stones within the building of God, that is the Body of Christ. Anything God does in us that isn't pressed into a deeper relationship with His family is incomplete. There is no success within God's Kingdom apart from the family. ***His grace...is able to build you up and give you an inheritance among all who are sanctified.***[197]

HABITATION

Just as monetary wealth cannot create richness for someone who is alone, and perfect health cannot be exercised by someone without any time to live, so it is with spiritual development. If you claim spiritual growth or realization separate from the ability to express and share it with others, if that "growth" has been gotten outside of a shared experience in which others sowed into your harvest, then whatever it is you think you have hulled will be found lacking the power to reproduce. In essence, your harvest is dead before it even has a chance to live.

If we never come, as living stones, into fellowship with the Body of Christ in a deep, selfless, and *truly* godly way, we have missed the entire point of walking even a step on the one bloody road of discipleship.

There was a time in history where all the Church had was each other, the Spirit of God, and the living Gospel. There are places even now, places in the world where identifying as a "Christian" carries with it the sentence of isolation, persecution, and death. I have been to some of those places. I have looked into the eyes of those whose families

---

[197] Derived from Acts 20:32.

have rejected them, who no longer have a people in the earth who stand with them. I speak of people who have no prospects for a "better life," simply because they love the same Jesus I do. As I sit and edit this text, I am flying into a city some forty miles from the operational capital of ISIS where I will spend just a week alongside giants—hidden titans of faith who have truly staked all they have on the Gospel—tasting of the cup they share with their wives and kids on behalf of the Lord.

In these places no quarrel over useless nonsense sets the tone for the religious board meetings that govern our chubby churches. In those previous days, persecuted ones didn't have the luxury of quibbling over obscure Scripture and the value of each other's doctrinal positions. I speak of ones, who with the breath they have, spend themselves "redeeming the time,"[198] as Paul exhorted, in the desire that every moment they are afforded in this life would be full of experience with the living Christ and His love in their midst. In these places people who have nothing willingly offer the little luxuries they gather to host guests, to reach out to ones even more desperate than they are, and in worship of the God who has graced them with life.

This is the expression of love for which Christ died. This—not the size of our gatherings, or the quality of our lighting, or the grandeur of our worship band—is how God is really displayed. No, not even how many people we feed or churches we plant testifies of the love of Christ. As Stephen the first-century martyr declared, "...the Most High does not dwell in houses made of hands...."[199]

Only selflessness and humility prepare the ground for a habitation that serves as the space for a move of God that shakes the foundations of the world. I am not talking about

---

[198] See Ephesians 5:16-18.
[199] Acts 7:48 (ESV)

revivals that come and go. I am speaking of the resting of God both upon and within a people—the sons and daughters of God taking their place in the world. This is the breeding ground for an atmosphere of signs, wonders, and miracles that do more than make a temporary noise. This kind of habitation can flow only as the by-product of love for God and His creation. This is the glory the Church has been fashioned to offer in our one universal ministry of reconciliation. "***Heaven is my throne, and the earth is my footstool. What kind of house will you build for me, says the Lord...***"[200]

* * *

On that day when physical death frees me into the glorified life of resurrection in Christ, I will call the crowd of witnesses together, climb right onto my Father's lap, and ask them all if things went anything like I picture them in the days after Christ ascended. In my mind, what I imagine to hear will be a story something like this...

"I *know* this isn't over. He said to come here and wait. I know He's doing something big. That gift He spoke of from the Father, it *must be special,*" Peter said.

"Was that a question, Peter?" James replied. "Ask my brother what he thinks. John always understood the Master best."

Both Peter and James had turned to John, not yet the Revelator, but nonetheless bound to Christ by a revelatory love they all were just beginning to taste. "I just get the sense He's not done building. Peter, you remember what He said to you...*He would build His Church...*He said the gates of hell would not win against it."

---

[200] See Stephen's message before being stoned in Acts 7; this from the ESV.

"Yeah," Peter said, a chuckle barely slipping out, "I'll never forget those words. That was a minute before He called me Satan." Again he grinned, this time finishing with a drawn-out breath of reflection. "I'd do almost anything to hear Him speak to me like that again."

"No, Peter, wait...I think it all is starting to make sense!" James was sitting upright now, tying John's heart to the words of Christ, of which Peter always seemed to bear the biggest blows. "Think about what He said, 'Only the Father could have shown us He was the Messiah...I will build my church...and hell will not prevail against it.' He told us to wash each other, and then—then on the beach... Peter, he told you to go and feed His children!"

They were onto it now, as James was connecting the dots. Jesus always told them they wouldn't understand until after He was gone. Now, as they waited in Jerusalem with the rest of the disciples and the hundred or so others who had followed Him through His ascension to heaven, things were coming into focus. "Remember what happened, just before the moment He went up to the Father. I can see it! *We* are it! He *is* building! He's building the temple that He said He would tear down! *He's building it with...US!*"

"And He opened their understanding, that they might comprehend the Scriptures. Then He said to them,

> 'Thus it is written, and thus it was necessary for the Christ to suffer and to rise from the dead the third day, and the repentance and remission of sins should be preached in His name to all nations, beginning at Jerusalem.... Behold, I send you the promise of My Father upon you....'"[201]

---

[201] Luke 24:45-49

John finally put it all together. "What about when He breathed on us...When He appeared to us in the house. Do you remember His words to us *then*?" Peter and James nodded. 'Receive the Holy Spirit,' He said. If you forgive people's sins, they are forgiven.... But then He said, if we hold onto their sins, those sins would indeed be held." As John finished speaking, Peter was staring right into John's eyes.

"Priests. He has given us the job of priests," Peter said.

"Yeah," John replied. "He gave us His Spirit, the Spirit that has only lived in the Temple...*and Him.*" They were all frozen as Christ's words rested on them in power.

And just then Peter spoke these words, as if directly to the Lord in heaven above, "Though they desire to kill us, though we may hang just as You did, You have commissioned us to forgive them in the same way You have forgiven us. And just as sure as I walked on the water, I declare before You, Lord, and my brothers, that I...*will spend my life to set them free!*"

Then, seemingly out of nowhere, the curtains began to stir.

The sound of a mighty, rushing wind filled the room...

...and with it cloven tongues as of fire descended upon each of their heads.[202]

In a flash like wind and fire, the Church was born....

THE END IS THE BEGINNING

There is only one place for this to end. The conclusion to my message is the only message which has any power. There is only one message with any true value beyond what will rot and perish, and it is the only place where we can

---

[202] Adapted from events described in the conclusion of the gospels, and the first two chapters of Acts.

find hope and life. I beckon all who would, to come to the fountain that never runs dry. I call on all who have ears to hear, to submit themselves to the Gospel, take the hand of Jesus, and walk the One Bloody Road of true discipleship.

We will never compete with the world's display of "worldly" success. I wish we would stop trying. I desire with all of my heart and life that the people of God in the earth would grow up in the way we act, while staying like innocent children in our relationship to sin,[203] so that the world would know *we are* different. We will never save the world by making the Christ they crucified nice enough, inviting enough, or self-gratifying enough for them to join up and follow Him. They would hang Him again.

> **We will never save the world by making the Christ they crucified nice enough.**

The ones who long for more will come where more is to be found. More is found in the source of abundant life. More isn't just a quantifiable amount above what they have, with a better good-to-evil ratio and the right language. More is only found in Christ.

Though this road has no end, the destination is the very One who has walked it before you. Jesus Christ—beaten, bloodied, and crucified—has made a way for you to pass through every trial and test this life has to offer, and to be resurrected in glory, just as He was. In the process, along that bloody road, if you will allow Him to do it, the glorified Son will take you to places you never imagined. He will take you beyond the ritual of religion, pull you up above whatever heights your mind can dream up, and draw you into a rest that steadies even the quietest recesses of the universe.

---

[203] See 1 Corinthians 14:20.

God, *your loving Father,* will show you things this world does not understand, things your heart longs for, as He welcomes you into the family of heaven which is advancing right here, in our world. There is no greater call, no higher value, and no more abundant life than the broken life of a living stone which sits upon Jesus, the Rock of Ages. I bid you to join with all of creation to reveal the glory of God until the day Christ returns for His pure and spotless bride. His eternal invitation to you was written in blood.

There is no better time than now to simply say, "I do."

> **I bid you to join with all of creation to reveal the glory of God until the day Christ returns.**

Epilogue

In light of all we have been through, and in testimony of where we now stand together before the Lord and His Word, I would like to depart from you, once again presenting a famous verse of Scripture. I pray that your encounter with the Gospel, your place as sons and daughters, your perseverance in brokenness, your experience in abundant life, and your dedication as living stones, is forever altered in a glorious walk with the Lord, as one with the heart of the psalmist...

The Lord is my shepherd;
I shall not want.
He makes me to lie down in green pastures;
He leads me besides the still waters.
He restores my soul;
He leads me in the paths of righteousness
For His name's sake.

Yea, though I walk through the valley
of the shadow of death,
I will fear no evil;
For You are with me;
Your rod and Your staff,
they comfort me.

You prepare a table before me
in the presence of my enemies;
You anoint my head with oil;
My cup runs over.

> *Surely goodness and mercy shall follow me*
> *all the days of my life;*
> *And I will dwell in the house of the Lord*
> *Forever.*

> —Psalm 23

More from Burning Ones...

These pages contain my heart, poured out for Jesus to see Him revealed in all the earth. Other than God's grace I count my greatest boast the gift He gave to me in Nikki, my beautiful wife of thirteen years at the time of writing this book. My single greatest achievement in this life is found in my wonderful children: Angelina, Nikki, Giuseppe, and Eliana.

Over more than a decade, I have served the Lord as a youth pastor, stood with my family as a missionary in Tanzania, and traveled the world declaring the Gospel. Whether on crusade platforms, or in dirty tents, I have walked in places where men far greater than I have ploughed the road. The one amazing thing I constantly encounter is God touching a broken life through the redemption of Christ. My prayer is that in all I do one legacy will remain; Jesus Christ lifted up in my place and the hearts of men and women won for the love of their Father through me.

For information regarding seminars, conferences, speaking or preaching engagements, or for missions training and/or trip opportunities, please visit my author site **jggarrettbooks.com**. Contacts or requests for "Invitation" authors of chapters 2-7 can be reached through the contact form at **jggarrettbooks.com**.

🐦 @AfricanJohnny
📷 @johnnyGrat
📘 #onebloodybook
onebloodybook@gmail.com
www.facebook.com/1bloodyroad

JGGARRETTBOOKS.COM
BURNINGONES.ORG
TOUCHINGNATIONSTODAY.ORG